Voices of Students

"When I talked to Mr. Riteman alone I said to him, 'You're a survivor, and most of all, you're my hero.'" – *Michael Smialek*

"I have never cried in school, not ever, until I heard Mr. Riteman speak. I have never been so touched or informed."
– *Melissa Brown*

"His words have changed my life forever." – *Norman Samaha*

"Mr. Riteman is wonderful for sacrificing his own preference to keep silent in favour of teaching the younger generations . . . lest we forget." – *Katie O'Connor*

"Some days when I'm having a bad day or think the week can't get any worse, I think about Mr. Riteman. Then I realize that things aren't as bad as I believe them to be." – *Emily Stachecki*

"I think the most powerful moment of Mr. Riteman's speech was when he looked around the auditorium and said through his tears, 'You are very lucky children.' Because we are. And we should never forget it." – *Kayla Andrews*

"I personally was touched by Mr. Riteman's speech. I have a new outlook on life, and realize my problems are miniscule compared to what this honourable man went through. It has made me a better person." – *Jason Warn*

D1260797

Millions of Souls

Millions of Souls

THE PHILIP RITEMAN STORY

as told to Mireille Baulu-MacWillie

FLANKER PRESS LIMITED

ST. JOHN'S

2010

Library and Archives Canada Cataloguing in Publication

Riteman, Philip
    Millions of souls : the Philip Riteman story / as told to Mireille Baulu.

Includes index.
    ISBN 978-1-897317-78-5

 1. Riteman, Philip. 2. Auschwitz (Concentration camp). 3. World War,
1939-1945--Conscript labor--Germany. 4. World War, 1939-1945--
Concentration camps. 5. Holocaust, Jewish (1939-1945). 6. Holocaust,
Jewish (1939-1945)--Personal narratives. 7. Concentration camp inmates--
Biography. 8. Holocaust survivors--Canada--Biography. 9. World War,
1939-1945--Personal narratives, Jewish. 10. Polish Canadians--Biography.
I. Baulu-MacWillie, Mireille, 1940- II. Title.

D804.196.R58 2010   940.53'18092   C2010-905136-X

© 2010 by Philip Riteman

PRINTED IN CANADA

MIX
Paper from
responsible sources
FSC® C016245

This paper has been certified to meet the environmental and social standards of the Forest Stewardship Council® (FSC®) and comes from responsibly managed forests, and verified recycled sources.

Cover Design: Adam Freake

FLANKER PRESS   PO BOX 2522, STATION C   ST. JOHN'S, NL, CANADA
TOLL FREE: 1-866-739-4420
WWW.FLANKERPRESS.COM

10 9 8 7 6 5 4

Canada   Canada Council   Conseil des Arts   Newfoundland
         for the Arts   du Canada   Labrador

We acknowledge the [financial] support of the Government of Canada. *Nous reconnaissons l'appui [financier] du gouvernement du Canada.* We acknowledge the support of the Canada Council for the Arts, which last year invested $153 million to bring the arts to Canadians throughout the country. *Nous remercions le Conseil des arts du Canada de son soutien. L'an dernier, le Conseil a investi 153 millions de dollars pour mettre de l'art dans la vie des Canadiennes et des Canadiens de tout le pays.* We acknowledge the financial support of the Government of Newfoundland and Labrador, Department of Tourism, Culture and Recreation for our publishing activities.

I dedicate this book to my family
and to the millions who perished in the Holocaust.

CONTENTS

Preface

I MET PHILIP RITEMAN in October 2007 at a conference for educators during Holocaust Education Week. As a survivor, he was there to offer support to the organizers of the conference. I did not know anything about his life. However, meeting this man had a great impact on me because it was the first time in my life I was seeing a survivor with my own eyes. Since the age of thirteen, I had been reading about the Holocaust after my mother had given me *The Diary of Anne Frank* to read. It started me on a lifelong quest to learn what happened to millions and millions of people during the regime of the Third Reich. Those witnesses and saviours of Jews, the Righteous Among the Nations, who wrote about their experience provided me with an insight into the overwhelming cruelty of the Nazis, the resilience of persons surviving dehumanizing circumstances and the courage of those who risked their lives to save people who were facing a terrible fate.

After meeting Philip Riteman, I searched to see if his story had been written. It had not. Gathering my courage, I called him to ask if he would be interested in writing his story. His answer on the phone was not too encouraging, but he invited me to meet with him at his home. I accepted the invitation and, for two hours, he was not sure that he wanted to get involved in this project. I did not pressure him but indicated that if he changed his mind I would be willing to help him. At the end of the visit, he suddenly took the decision to tell his story and allow me to write it; for me this was a great responsibility and a very special privilege.

For six months we met once or twice a week and his story unfolded little by little. At times it was excruciating for him to reveal some of the horrors he saw and experienced. He would hold back very difficult memories for a while and then would make the decision to impart some of them. Sharing this heavy emotional burden constantly brought out his tears of loss and pain. To this day he sees more clearly than ever the tragedy brought about by the Nazi regime and feels that we cannot comprehend the experiences of survivors who had to bear the terrible brutality and murderous practices of the Nazis in the concentration camps.

However, one thing became obvious as I listened to him and attempted to be true to his voice; he felt that this book would strengthen the knowledge about the Holocaust and perhaps awaken the conscience of young people to create an outrage against all forms of genocide. Each experience of survival is different and has the potential to touch the human heart as his story touched mine. I will forever be grateful to Philip Riteman because he gave me a window through which I could see how surviving takes courage and determination.

MIREILLE BAULU-MACWILLIE

Millions of Souls

Introduction

"Hitler's butchery was something new, something never to be understood by anybody, and the human tongue is unable to express it properly."[1]

RUTH ALTBEKER CYPRYS

TERRIBLE THINGS HAPPENED TO me when I was young and I did not talk about them for forty years. I dreamt, talked to myself, and thought about them all the time: *Should I speak or should I not speak?* I was ashamed, I was frightened. I did not know what to say to people. I thought that they would think I was lying, that there was something wrong with me. I once spoke to my aunt about what happened to me. When I started to tell her, I cried. She said, "Oh my God, Philip is sick. I have to take him to the doctor." Once she even took me to a psychiatrist. She saw me cry, even though most of the time I used to go away and hide. There were a lot of things in my mind after I came to Newfoundland. The memories were very raw. I would think, *Am I living? Am I dreaming? Maybe I will go back and see my parents.* I thought that if I made a few dollars I would send the money to them. It was like a fantasy. Would I see my brothers? Would I see my sisters? In my head, in my dreams, in my thinking, I wondered if it really happened. I used to cry a lot. Even now I am still experiencing the same torturous memories and cry. How could this have happened to me, not only to me but to millions? I always think about it, even today. I still wonder if I will ever see my family again. When I was going around alone selling from door to door with a pack on my back in Newfoundland out in the country, I used to ask myself, "Is it true?" I would touch my skin to see if it was really me or if I was dreaming.

These words are from Philip Riteman, a Holocaust survivor of the extermination by the Nazis of a third of European Jewry and millions of other human beings. He is one who has seen with his own eyes and lived the experience of cruelty in its most horrific proportions. Driven out from his home as a teenager in Shershev[2], Poland and marched approximately forty miles to the town of Malch[3] before entering the Pruzhany[4] ghetto, he was then deported to Auschwitz-Birkenau and used as a forced labourer in five different concentration camps. There he lost his whole family and witnessed the cruelest treatments that can be inflicted on human beings: degradation, dehumanization, starvation, hard labour, daily beatings, torture and deliberate, cold-blooded murder. Against all odds, he managed to survive! He makes it his obligation today to speak to younger generations so that they can be instrumental in preventing something like this ever happening again. What follows is his story: a story of survival that begins in his teenage years, continues after his arrival in Newfoundland, and unfolds in the retelling today of the events he experienced in the concentration camps.

In 1939, Poland was invaded by Germany, which already occupied extensive territories. At about the same time, the Russians had taken over an eastern part of Poland that they called Belarus and had stayed a little more than a year. One of Philip's older brothers was conscripted in the Russian[5] Army and was stationed near Smolensk. When the Russians overtook this part of the country, they did not bother the Jews; they were simply anti-business. Philip's hometown of Shershev was in that area as part of the Pruzhany district. Its population was approximately eighteen to twenty thousand people, between two to five thousand of which were Jews. When the Germans conquered this part of Poland, the Russians had to retreat. It appeared that some Russian soldiers had not followed their units.

The Germans rounded up six or seven of these deserters in the wetlands near the town and the townspeople heard the shooting. Had they been there they would also have been shot. It was said that these Russians had been killed because the Germans would not take prisoners. The knowledge that they did not take prisoners encouraged some Russians to run away to the woods and become partisans.

In June 1941, nearly one million German soldiers marched day and night through Shershev on their way to Russia with their tanks, trucks, and munitions. If people were seen on the street by the soldiers, they were killed, Jews or Gentiles. Civilians knew that war was in full force but did not know what to expect. They did not even realize that the Germans were going from town to town expelling the people. If somebody had told them what was happening, they would not have believed it. Nobody wanted to believe this kind of thing. For the Jews as well as the Christians, it would be their last months of a normal life in their village.

I remember my childhood as being happy and having friends of different religions: Jews, Catholics, Protestants, Orthodox, and Baptists. In the summer a group of us would go swimming and fishing in the river as well as going horseback riding. We would take blankets outside and all go lie down and sleep. We visited each other's houses, ate and slept there. In the winter we went skating on the river together. Our skates were not like the ones today. They were made by hand from wood. Our area was farmland. The farmers would take pieces of wood and shape them as skates to fit on our shoes. These would be tied with rope. On the bottom there was a long and very sharp piece of steel that was bolted to the skate. In Russian, we used to call them *dropky*. We would go skating for many miles. Sometimes we would prepare lunch and go away for the whole day. In some places, they sold drinks in little huts. Some people would even give us drinks without charging us. We skated when the lights came on. That was fun for us. When I came to Newfoundland and took my children skating, I put on a pair of skates and surprised my wife that I could skate. During the month of May in our town government officials, the Army, civil servants, policemen and firemen would march along the town accompanied by Polish music and songs. As children we followed them and felt it was a very special time.

My family consisted of my mother, my father, six boys and two girls. I was the fourth child. I also had an extended family consisting of grandparents, nine aunts and uncles and many cousins. We belonged to a community that had many different Christian religions. Christians and Jews got along well; they were friends, and they bought and sold goods and produce to each other. In 1937–1938 we heard rumours of war and, before the Germans actually came, propaganda against

Jews extended to our area: "Hate the Jews! Hate the Jews!" Lamentably it caused people that had nothing against the Jews to start hating them. There were cartoons published in the newspapers depicting Jews with long crooked noses, pointed ears, witches' eyes, and long nails as if they wanted to eat people alive. These portrayals made the Jews look more like devils than human beings.

Classmates with whom I went to school did not see any differences between their own facial features and those of the Jews and would wonder why these drawings were published. However, propaganda has a way of changing people's mindset and Jewish children started to be taunted by the non-Jewish ones who even threw stones at them. In public school, teachers became anti-Semitic, but refrained from showing it too much, even when classmates would say, "You Jews, why don't you go to Palestine?" It was for lack of education that the Christians started to believe in the propaganda. When they talked about war in school, I came home one day and asked my father "Is there a war coming? What is the fighting for?" My father looked at me sadly and said, "I can't explain it to you. You are too young to understand."

CHAPTER ONE

Leaving Shershev

WHEN THE GERMAN ARMY passed through the town, a group of soldiers stopped on the road near our house and I saw them using the water in the well to shave themselves. One of them said to me, "Russia is *kaputt* (gone), England is *kaputt* and all the Jews are *kaputt*. Germany will conquer the world." I went in the house to convey this to my mother and she forbade me to talk to the soldiers. A couple of days later, while the soldiers were still marching through Shershev, my older brother went to the market square and came running back home through the meadows, crying and telling my parents that the Germans were shooting people on the street. My father did not believe it and said, "They cannot kill innocent people." Not long after, sometime in September after the harvest, another group of Germans called the *Einsatzgruppen* came to our town. The soldiers called on the mayor and the councillors and told them that all the Jews from now on would have to wear the yellow Star of David on their clothes. Then they rounded up the few policemen of the town and made them give up their guns. Finally they gave the mayor and the councillors the order to collect ten kilos of gold and twenty kilos of silver. The councillors went to every house, Jewish as well as Gentile, and asked for gold and silver, which could be any kind of jewellery such as necklaces, rings, or earrings. They told the people that they had to give these to the Germans.

One councillor came to our house. He was not Jewish, but he had been beaten up by the Nazis, who had told all the councillors that if they were not going to collect this gold and silver they would all be killed. I saw the bruised face of the man and asked my mother what had happened to him. My mother told me to leave them and she would tell me later. She gave the man her earrings, her wedding ring and a few gold coins belonging to my father. She also gave him our silver cutlery. All these precious objects were collected from around the town and given to the Nazis. My father didn't mind giving them to the Germans. He didn't care, as long as they would leave people alone. After that, the

Germans disappeared, and their departure calmed the people.

However, a couple of days later, the *Einsatzgruppen* came back and demanded double the amount of gold and silver. Of course people did not have it, so the Germans surrounded the town with many soldiers and trucks. They were coming to get all the Jews, but they did not know where their houses were. Jewish families lived right alongside Gentile families, but were in the minority. Some Germans found out because prisoners had been taken out of the jail and were revealing the locations of Jewish homes. The Christians were frightened and did nothing to save the Jews. In fact when the Germans were finished with the Jews they killed many Christians. We were told that policemen, lawyers and doctors had been murdered. According to some people, a few had survived.

That very same day at two or three o'clock in the morning, I heard banging at our door. I went to open it because I was the one who slept the closest to it. My brothers probably had not heard the first banging. But the noise woke up the family. Everyone was wondering what was happening. When the door was opened, we all saw a Nazi with a gun yelling, "*Raus, raus, raus, verfluchte Juden* (Out, out, out, cursed Jews)!" They told us to get dressed and they marched us to a big square. There was not only my family in the square but numerous Jewish families as well that lived in the town.

There were lights on the square because it was four or five o'clock in the morning. It took awhile, until daylight, to finally round up all the Jews of Shershev. Then, soldiers came with horses and buggies. They took the children, the women, and the older men away in these buggies.

The males from twelve years of age to approximately fifty years were marched out of the town accompanied by the German soldiers and their German shepherd dogs. They were riding on bicycles, motorcycles, or in army trucks. In my eyes there were probably more than a thousand that marched. In the group there was a man I knew. His name was Mandel and he was about forty years old. I went to school with one of his daughters. Suddenly he was taken to the side of the road and was told to kneel down on a log. A German took his revolver and shot him in the head. We had been ordered to watch and were frightened to death. I was about fifty feet away from him and saw him jerk. It was the first time I witnessed a man being shot. The shooting of people on the way was for me a traumatic experience.

We walked approximately forty miles to the town of Malch. Most of the people around there would have been farmers, but the Germans were killing farmers. It was a region that had a lot of cattle which the Germans had taken away. When you are a teenager, there are so many things you don't understand so you cling to your family. But I felt lost because some members of my family had been separated from me. During the march they started shooting at people that I knew. They shot the bus driver that used to go from Shershev to Pruzhany and back. His father came screaming and yelling at the German who had done that: "Why did you kill my son? He didn't do anything." The soldier shot the father also, and they both were buried in a grave on the roadside. They also killed over a hundred people during that march.

Before they let us go, they brought us to a field which had little ravines. They took fourteen men and made them dig a big pit. One of them was my neighbour. He used to have a little shop and he gave us candy when we were children. They made these men undress, leaving them only with their underwear. Then they positioned them at the edge of that pit. One of the images that haunt me to this day is of standing near the men behind a German soldier, having been asked to hold his bicycle. He and many other soldiers first killed seven of these men by shooting them in the back of the head. Their bodies tumbled in what would become their grave. The soldiers then proceeded to kill the seven others in the same manner. They covered the bodies with earth, but one could still see movement under there. So the soldiers added a lot more soil, jumped on top of it and started pumping bullets in the ground. In general, people have no idea of how scared one gets seeing such things. That was real fear.

After this episode, the Germans left our group and went away. As we walked toward the nearby village of Malch, we saw bushes that must have been three or four feet high at the far end of the field. According to a long tradition, farmers planted these bushes to divide the land. Strangely, we realized that behind those bushes there were people talking. We were stunned to find the people from our village who had been taken away in the buggies. They were standing or sitting on the ground because the Germans had taken away the horses and buggies. I sought the members of my family and found them. I gave them a warm hug. My little sister was crying and I started to cry with her. I asked, "What happened to you?" They answered that they had been brought to this place but that on the way the Germans had killed many people. They named this one and that one who had been killed. In our town everybody knew everybody.

One lady had a little boy. He was a bit simple, and they shot him. She also had a little girl of about six years old. This lady was screaming at the Nazis, "Why did you kill him? He didn't do anything." They responded by killing her and her little girl. After this event, the soldiers disappeared and left the people there. As a group we then decided to walk into the little village. In this village there was a small church. We discovered that the village was completely empty. We would go into homes and there was not a soul in these places. I felt like ghosts were grabbing me and I said to my father, "I am not going to stay here." My father answered, "No, we are going back home." Sadly, after being taken out of my town, I never went back and saw it again.

CHAPTER TWO

From the Pruzhany Ghetto to Auschwitz

THE GROUP DECIDED TO go from Malch back in the direction of Shershev, which passed by the town of Pruzhany. My mother was born in that town. Her brother and her parents lived there. Also, my father had a brother and a sister with large families whose homes were in Pruzhany. On the road we saw many German cars and the soldiers were shooting at us. So we hid in the woods and walked at night. From the leftovers of the harvest in the fields we found food: carrots, cabbage and potatoes. For water we drank with our bare hands as we passed some streams. After walking for four or five days, our parents figured that they could stay in Pruzhany with some of our family. Pruzhany was a big town and it had different neighbourhoods, some very nice ones and some older ones not as nice and rather poor. Christians and Jews lived side by side in all these sections. The Germans had taken out the Christians from the older neighbourhoods and had formed a ghetto for the Jews. They had also surrounded the newly created area with barbwire. They took away all the nice homes owned by Jews, one of these belonging to my aunt, and displaced their owners and their families in the ghetto. All the Jews who lived in Pruzhany were moved to the ghetto, as well as those who were arriving from the surrounding area. In the ghetto, my family was given just three rooms. Each one had a surface of about twelve by fifteen feet. We shared these rooms with my mother's brother, a family of two adults and five children, as well as with my maternal grandparents. It was crowded and we had only one little wood stove for all of us. So we all ate together. Furthermore, we lived like hungry rats because of the food and wood shortages.

My brother who was in the Russian Army was captured by the Germans when they marched into Russia. He succeeded in escaping them, took off his uniform and mingled with civilians. After a few months on the run, he joined us in the Pruzhany ghetto. His escape is a story in itself, of living off the land and hiding in all kinds of places.

I can't talk much about the ghetto, but the time I spent there was not a happy one. At night, along with other teenagers, I would lift up the barbwire and crawl out like a snake to go into the fields and little wooded areas to find something to eat and wood for the stove. We were only teenagers and some of us got shot. As well, the Germans came and rounded those who were between twelve and twenty years of age. They took us to places where our tasks consisted of working on farms, cutting trees and fixing roads. We would stay a week or ten days where they took us before going back to the ghetto. It was hard labour. Some of the young people would just run away. When they started to run, we heard *Bing, Bing, Bing*. It was the Germans who were shooting at them, and these young fellows never came back to the ghetto. When we returned to the ghetto after working on farms, we would bring back food and the Germans let us do it. They pretended not to see us. Once a group of workers was brought back, the Germans needed replacements for them. I saw soldiers catching people, beating them and taking them away for the hard labour.

Some people were suspected of having contacts with the partisans. However, even if a person had no contact with them, the Germans would accuse them of it and carry on their senseless murders. I was told that when they caught partisans they would tie them up together, torture them and then kill them, although I did not see that with my own eyes. At that time I did not know that I would have to personally experience Nazi cruelty in a much more systematic and extensive way.

Even if my memory is not clear on this fact, it is documented that the liquidation of the Pruzhany ghetto took place in January 1943. The Germans took sections of the ghetto one at a time, men, women and children. They went to each door and said, "We have to send you out on farms." People said, "On farms it is cold in the winter, but we will survive the war. There must be homes." In the beginning, my father believed this. He said, "Thank God, at least we are freer on a farm. We can get outdoors." The Germans told us that we could take whatever we wanted. Since we didn't know where we were going, some took valuables, money and, for the little children, a loaf of bread or a bottle of water. We walked from the ghetto to the Lineve train station, driven by the Germans. I don't remember it as being cold and there was just a little bit of wet snow on the ground. We all wore coats or sheepskin jackets.

My eyes could not see far enough to know how many freight cars there were. However, there were many and the Germans ran around with rifles, shooting in the air trying to frighten us, and driving us *"Schnell, schnell, schnell* (Fast, fast, fast)."* It was a few miles to the railway station. Then they packed each freight car with approximately eighty to one hundred human beings, including men, women and children. If one can imagine, we were packed like sardines and were not even able to sit or lie on the floor to rest. They told us the trip would last one hour in the country, and after they would let us go. They lied to us. We believed them because we never imagined what they were going to do to us. We were so packed in the freight car that if I wanted to turn around I could not. They had closed the train, boxing us in. We heard shooting. I don't know if they were killing people with their rifles.

Finally the train left the station, very slowly. After an hour, it kept on going. It did not stop and everybody was waiting. Two hours went by and the train still kept on going slowly. We thought that they were going to let us out. We looked out through the openings between the boards and we saw fields and homes far away. We heard the whistle of the train. If I hear the whistle of a train today, it reminds me of that trip and gives me shivers. We could only stand up at all times. We could not sit down. Everybody was shaking with the movement of the train. There was no food, no water, and no toilet. One man dropped dead at my feet. A fellow behind me said, "Maybe you can try to move the man with your feet." And that is how we pushed his body to the wall. And the train kept on going at about twenty miles an hour, clickety-click, clickety-click, often stopping for a few hours before starting again. At the end of our car there was a fellow who pushed a little spoon through the boards to collect rain or snow in order to have a bit of water.

One very pretty lady, in her twenties had a baby in her arms in our freight car. The baby started crying. I can still hear him now. He cried all day and all night. Early in the morning, at daylight, the baby stopped crying. Unfortunately he had died in her arms and she became hysterical. A man behind me wanted to take the baby from her, but she would not give it up. She was screaming. She was bewildered. He finally succeeded and put the baby's dead body on the other body. Despair was setting in. People were moaning, screaming and yelling. They were peeing and shitting in their clothes. The screams, the smell, oh my God, I will never forget this. It seemed to me that it took many days before the arrival at our destination and it felt like forever. I thought we were going to die on that train.

One early morning, after daylight had just broken, we saw lights on top of long poles from the freight car, and the train started to slow down. Looking out through the boards of our enclosure, we saw a big inscription on which was written ARBEIT MACHT FREI (WORK MAKES YOU FREE) over a gate at the entrance of a large property. Across from the train there was a sign indicating Auschwitz-Birkenau. As it slowed down, the train was following a very long concrete platform until it finally stopped. Then the doors of the freight cars were opened and people were able to get out. I helped my little sister, who was about six or seven years old. My younger brother followed and my older sister assisted my mother getting down. My father and other brothers jumped out of the train after that. With all the commotion of people getting off the train, the dead bodies left in the freight cars were taken away by prisoners of the camp with striped clothes who had to work for the Germans. On the platform there were what appeared to be thousands of men, women, and children completely confused about where they were. The place appeared in total chaos.

I looked around and, in the freight car ahead of ours, there was a girl who jumped out on the platform. She was carrying a baby in her arms. I will never forget this. She was very pretty and wore high-heeled shoes. A German grabbed her baby out of her arms and threw it on a pile of babies already on the ground. A little while later, I was going to find out what was to happen to those babies. In the meantime the young woman was hysterical, wild like a beast. The German pushed his bayonet into her stomach and she fell to the ground. I saw blood running out of her. I jumped over her because I didn't want to fall on top of her. Just then I got hit over the head because they had told me to go to a wall. Before doing so I ran to say goodbye to my family, from which they had separated me. I grabbed my father and mother and gave them a hug. A German soldier told me, "You will see them tomorrow." I did not see them the next day. How could I have known then that I would never see them again? They were sent to the gas chambers, but I did not know at the time that there were such things as gas chambers and crematoriums.

On that platform I saw a man with a bad leg. He

seemed to be a nice man. I don't know if he was Jewish or not because he had just come in like me to this camp, but walked with a limp. A German took a revolver and shot him behind the head and the man fell. We were all standing there. I felt numbed. The poor man was not old, maybe in his fifties. Today we would call him a young man. I will never forget him. I don't know what his nationality or his religion was. I often dream about him. They took his life just because he could not walk well. There was no hope for someone with a disability. That person would be sent to the line of those who were going directly to the gas chambers.

There were thousands of people who had disembarked from that train onto the platform and no one knew what would happen. All those babies who had been thrown on the ground were screaming and crying. I can hear the babies crying even now. All of a sudden, I saw Germans starting to beat the babies on the head to silence them. What happened after I did not witness. I was so confused, mesmerized, I could not understand what was happening to me. However I asked what had happened and was told by others that a truck suddenly appeared. The babies had died as a result of being beaten. A few Germans came with pitchforks, hooked the babies by their diapers and threw them aboard the truck, which left with its heart-wrenching load. I could not help saying to myself, "Oh my God, what the hell is this all about?"

We were standing like sticks. Prisoners who were working for the Germans yelled, "Make yourself older!" And a fellow behind me said to me, "How old are you?" I answered, "I am a teenager. What business is it of yours how old I am?" He said, "Say you are eighteen." I looked at him. I didn't know the man, even though he came on the same train as mine. He was in his thirties, between thirty and thirty-five. A moment later, a German walked over toward me and said, "How old are you?" I answered, "I am eighteen." Later I realized that following the man's advice and lying about my age may have saved my life. Hearing my answer, the German said, "Go there to this wall." I ran, but he called me back and asked me, "What is your profession?" A fellow near me said, "He is a locksmith mechanic." I knew how to be a locksmith mechanic like I knew how to get to the moon. But, I said yes. That was the beginning of lying to the Germans in order to survive.

Many people from the train, maybe two or three hundred, were asked what their profession was. If they answered that they were a teacher, a judge, an accountant, a policeman, a lawyer, a doctor, an engineer or a faculty professor, they were sent to another wall. Then the Germans came with their machine guns from both sides and killed them right on the spot. But if persons said they were a bricklayer, a farmer, a shoemaker, a dressmaker, a candlestick maker, whatever work the Germans needed, these persons, provided they were young and strong, would not be shot. Professionals, most women and children they had no need for and they got rid of them. Now, being thought of as a worker who would be useful to the Germans, I was soon to learn what life as a slave labourer in a concentration camp was to be. My two older brothers were also among those chosen for this kind of work.

We were taken to a barracks where everybody had to take off their clothes. We were stark naked. They had taken everything from us: clothes, shoes, rings, watches, jewels and money. Later on, they even took gold teeth out of people's mouths. Anyone who was found to have gold teeth did not live very long. With nothing left on us, they proceeded to shave all the hair on our bodies. They even spread our buttocks with a stick and shaved us there. I did not have much hair, except on my head, but they shaved me anyway. They had a bucket with some kind of disinfecting solution and a big wool glove that they dipped in it. With this solution, they gave us a smear on the parts of the body that had been shaven. The combination of shaving our skin and dousing us with this mixture burned our flesh. When that was finished we had to stand up straight. A soldier came with a flashlight, looked up our arse, and opened our mouth to check that nothing was hidden. A man got shot on the spot for having a string sticking out of his anus, at the end of which was a hidden diamond. It was terrible. Besides, we were shivering from the cold, as it was the month of January. Something that was appalling to me as a teenager was seeing naked men peeing on the floor.

A partition made of walls was then opened and we had to run to the showers. I fell twice, the concrete floor being a sheet of ice. We were naked, we had no clothes, and they let the cold water run over us. People don't know what it means to be showered with cold, cold water. We were frozen to the bone.

They then opened up another door and we had to run out. On the way, they gave us a package of clothes consisting of shoes made of wood soles with cloth on top, a jacket, a shirt, a pair of pants and a cap. There was no underwear. They also gave us a red enamel bowl about six inches high and ten inches in diameter. I was to find out that a bowl is very important in a concentration camp. Without it you are dead. We used it for all our needs, not only eating. Still without our clothes on, we had to stop at a wicket and push our arm in it. Someone on the inside held my arm and tattooed a number on it with an old-fashioned pen and a bottle of ink. My number was 98706. Blood came out, but I did not care because I was so tired, not having slept for many days on the train. I could just as well have been dead. That number is still very visible today on my left arm. Then we all put our clothes on, but did no longer recognize each other. These clothes were made of a cloth that had stripes, and we could not bend our shoes. The noise as we walked sounded like *clump, clump* and *clump*.

Dressed in these strange attires, we were taken to our barracks; mine and my two brothers' was Block 16. We slept in bunks. The bunks were three-tiered and measured about six by seven feet and there was only thirty inches between each tier. We had to sleep five or six in a single bunk on rough, rough lumber. They gave us two big blankets per bunk, but no pillows. One was for covering the boards, which were full of splinters, and another for covering ourselves in order to keep warm. One of my sleep mates had to pull a splinter from my flesh. There were times when we wanted to put both blankets on the boards and would argue about it. In spite of the blanket covering the bed boards, we mostly had to sleep with our clothes on. Even more troubling was the fact that we could not sleep on our back or on our stomach. There was not enough room. We had to sleep sideways and could not turn around alone. We all turned together like pancakes. In the night, if we had the need to urinate, there was no washroom. People started arguing and fighting. Nobody wanted to be the recipient of someone's urine coming from an inmate on top. There were Russian prisoners in the barracks who said, "Boys, mind yourselves, you have enamel bowls, so you pee in the bowl. You hold it until morning, and when you go outside you throw it out." We would fall asleep but we never really rested. I did not know at that time that the worst was yet to come.

When the gong rang at five in the morning, the doors

of the barracks were opened; we had to go outside with our bowls, stand straight and line up in rows. There were thousands of men all lined up in front of their barracks to be counted. They brought out those who had died during the night, put them in front of us, made a mark on each of them with blue chalk and counted them also. When the counting was over, they brought big barrels of hot water, which they called coffee. The colour was black and green and it was made with leaves, which we could see at the bottom of the barrel. We had to throw our urine out and use our unwashed enamel bowl to receive this mixture. A man with a big ladle was dishing out a little bit of the so-called coffee to each one of us, and that was breakfast. It was so bitter we could hardly drink it. But it did quench our thirst. I drank three quarters of it and with the rest I washed my eyes and fingers.

Then the Germans taught us how to march. God help us if we did not march properly. They kept us marching for about one week in the camp. That is all we did during the day, nothing else. I am convinced that we marched better than the soldiers. After learning how to march, we were given bricks to hold with our extended arms and hands in a straight and horizontal way. We could not lift our arms up or bring them down. They had to stay straight and we had to jump with these. Anybody that could not do this was beaten to death with sticks. It was one way of weeding out the weak ones.

At lunchtime, which was at about twelve noon, they

brought barrels again. This time these barrels contained soup. We could not wash our bowl because there was no water to do so. We used to lick it. When we received our ladle of soup, we could see frogs' legs, red snails, bugs, worms and some meat of a kind that we could not recognize. Sometimes, it was a thick barley soup in which there was food that appeared somewhat disgusting. Everybody would say, "Close your eyes and don't look at what you are eating." Other times, the soup was much too salty, which made prisoners very thirsty. And there was no water to give us. Actually, the water in Auschwitz-Birkenau was contaminated and some people who drank it got dysentery.

At night, we were given a small loaf of heavy, very black soggy bread. The fellow that was responsible for a group, some sort of a *Kapo,* had to cut the bread in slices for five or six people. Sometimes we had to slice it ourselves. The bread appeared to be made more of sawdust than flour. Often there was some dispute about how the knife was placed to ensure an equal amount for everyone. The slice was the size of two pieces of toast stuck together. Most prisoners would eat their bread right away. That is what I did. Others would save a piece to eat a couple of hours later or in the morning and put it in a little purse, like a pocket, that they had made with cloth and strings, and wrapped around their neck. Unfortunately, some hungry prisoner who could not sleep because of hunger would tear away this little purse and gobble up the bread of his fellow prisoner. A Russian fellow would say, "They can't take the bread from me when it is inside." We were always terribly hungry and our daily diet was one of deprivation and starvation. With this regimen, we finally had to join the other prisoners of the camp and go to work.

CHAPTER THREE

A Journey into Hell

USCHWITZ WAS THE NAME given to a complex consisting of three concentration camps near the town of Oœwiêcim in Poland. These camps were Auschwitz, Auschwitz-Birkenau and Buna, which was later called Auschwitz-Monowitz III. This complex is one of the most infamous concentration camps of World War II. It became the scene of starvation, forced labour, torture, hangings, mass shootings and killing of unimaginable numbers of human beings by gassing them and then either burning their bodies in crematoriums or burying them in large pits, especially at the beginning. Auschwitz-Birkenau, a death camp, was the largest in the Nazi regime. There were hun-

29

dreds of barracks, which in total contained at times around a hundred thousand inmates.

More than a million people who were considered enemies of the Reich or unfit to qualify as part of the German race were brought to Auschwitz-Birkenau by train from all over Europe. Prime victims were the Jews (from different nationalities: Poles, Soviets, Czechs, Italians, Greeks, Dutch, French . . .), Jehovah's Witnesses, Romas, disabled persons, criminals and prisoners of war. There were also Catholics, Protestants and Orthodox in Auschwitz. Their presence there was not necessarily always because of their religion, but because of their opposition to the regime or their actions to save Jews.

When trainload after trainload full of people arrived, their "passengers" were dispossessed of all their belongings and selections were made. These selections were done by separating the people into two groups: those who were deemed able to work because they had useful trades for the Nazis, and those who didn't. Men, women and children who were of the latter category were immediately sent to the gas chambers where they were murdered and their bodies burned in crematoriums or buried in large pits. The crematoriums were active day and night at a rate that went as high as many thousands a day.

After its inception, the camp increased in size and expanded the number of its crematoriums. The wooden barracks, which housed at peak times perhaps as many as a thousand prisoners, were approximately two hundred feet long by fifty feet wide: usually about five hundred inmates in three- or four-tiered bunks on each long side. There was something that we called a chimney right across the whole length of the barracks floor. Inmates would sit on the chimney for a few minutes to put their shoes on or do something else. The camp was surrounded by three successive high-voltage electrified barbed-wire fencing. The first fence in the inside was about ten feet high. It had a wooden sign that read BE CAREFUL DON'T TOUCH, which was accompanied by the figure of a skull. This fence was separated from the second one by a space maybe fifteen feet across. This space was covered with beach stones. The second fence was higher than the first one and measured about twenty feet in height. A second space similar to the first one separated it from the third fence. This third fence was the highest and could have been fifty or sixty feet high.

If a prisoner was caught doing something that the Germans considered wrong, they would put him between the two first fences a whole day and a whole night as a twenty-four-hour punishment. The problem for the prisoner was that he could walk, sit or lie on the stones but could not touch the fences on either side of him without been electrocuted. Like many prisoners, Philip had to go there once.

However, he stayed only six or seven hours, being told to go to work in the morning. When some prisoners could not stand it anymore, they would throw themselves on the barbed wires as a quick way to end their lives. Along those fences there were towers higher than the highest fence. Guards were standing in them ready at all times to shoot with machine guns if it became necessary. At night there were beaming floodlights. All this was set up to prevent the escape of prisoners.

Each barracks had two doors, both barred at night by wood planks measuring two by four that hung on hooks across the doors. A guard stood at each door. There were no toilets in Auschwitz-Birkenau. The place to defecate was right in the open, in between the barracks, in a ditch parallel to the building. This ditch, about four of five feet deep, had a low cement wall for prisoners to sit and have their bowel movements. If a prisoner overstayed his time, a German would push him in the ditch with the flow. That meant sure death. To void their bladders, prisoners used their bowls or would do it anywhere. Today Auschwitz-Birkenau remains a vivid testimony of the strategic and systematic manner in which German anti-Semitic and racist policies deprived human beings of their dignity and annihilated more than a million people, the majority of which were Jewish.

After learning how to march in Auschwitz-Birkenau, and not knowing if we would survive, we were given the task to build a crematorium. None of us knew we were working on such a sinister project. They told us we were building a bakery that would bake bread. The way we had to do the work was to turn our jackets around so that they would be tied in our backs. Then we lifted the bottom part of the jacket in the front so that a fellow could load it with bricks, sand, or other materials that we would carry to the building site. It is hard to imagine several thousand people walking back and forth with their loads and sometimes dropping them on the ground. If a prisoner should unfortunately drop his load, he would not live very long and there were many who perished for this ill-fated accident. When I was working there, I saw my mother's brother, my uncle Shalom (Sam). We only looked at each other without saying a word. I also saw his son, my cousin Yankel (Jack). Neither one survived. My two brothers did not live through the ordeal either.

They had lied to us about what we were doing, and we believed them. I only found out about the gas chambers and the crematoriums after I had been in the camp for two weeks. I would ask about my family, and one of my co-workers wanted to know on what transport I had come. I showed my number and, when he saw it, he told me that they had been gassed and their bodies had gone up in smoke. Even after one month I still could not believe it. Finally I realized it when people said, "Smell it." The smoke had a strong and sweet smell of burning flesh that could be detected for maybe ten miles.

However, they could not incinerate the bodies fast enough in the two or three crematoriums running at that time. Piles of bodies had been left outside the crematoriums. I knew some inmates who had to dig pits of approximately ten feet deep, fifty or sixty feet long and twenty-five feet wide. They took the bodies from the crematoriums, loaded them up in wheelbarrows and ran across the yard, nearly a mile away, to bury them in the pits that had been dug. Then lime was poured over the bodies. They showed us the wooded area where these bodies had been buried. Most of the victims were women, older men of fifty and more, disabled persons, and children.

With a large crew, my turn came to work in a similar situation. I was pushing a wheelbarrow while others were loading it with dead bodies: men, women and children, most of them women and children. Again, because at that time there were not enough crematoriums to burn all the corpses, we had to walk to a forest to dump the bodies down in holes that had been dug. These pits measured what seemed to be ten or maybe twenty feet wide and a hundred feet long. There were piles and piles of bodies in there. They gave us metal buckets and we filled them with lime to spread over the bodies. I only worked there for a couple of days because I got sick and vomited and they had to take me away. The smell was horrific. Fellows before me had done the same thing. I didn't know what I had to do when I went there to work. Back at their barracks, a few of these fellows who had done this work hung themselves with their belts because, understandably, they could not take it. Upon seeing these suicides, the Germans took all our belts away.

When I was doing that gruesome work, I pretended that I didn't see it, even though I cannot forget the sight of it, and particularly the image of two tiny babies and children who were no more than five or six years old. I still cry when I think about it. I do not have the words to express the terrible deeds inflicted on all the innocent people that had to suffer such a fate. There would not be enough pens and ink in the world to write about all the senseless murders of the Nazi regime.

Sometime later, I worked with a crew of five hundred men carrying rails to build a railway. Those rails were heavy and extremely cold in the winter. The Germans would assign one or two dozen men to carry these big long rails of steel. We walked a couple of miles before laying them down for others to fasten them to the wood ties. We then had to go back to get more. The steel rails were so cold and we had to lift them up with our bare hands. The result was that these rails stuck to our flesh and the skin would come off leaving our hands very raw and in pain. To solve the problem we had to use paper from cement bags to carry these rails. I worked there for about three weeks. It was hard work for me and I was cold and starving. I did not want to work there. I happened to meet a fellow prisoner with whom I had walked to work. I asked him if I could work with him. He said, "Sure, I will ask my *Kapo*." *Kapos* were inmates in the camps who were responsible at times for as many as a thousand men. They would take the prisoners to their work sites. The *Kapo* agreed and said that I could move to another assignment. So long as a person could have the approval of the *Kapo*, he could change the work he was doing. Apart from this situation, prisoners were regularly shifted around for all the work that had to be done.

From Auschwitz-Birkenau we went to the Auschwitz concentration camp a couple of miles away. This concentration camp was more modern in appearance than the one we just left. The roads were paved and they had sidewalks. Its blocks were made of bricks and looked like old-fashioned hotels with regular windows. They had two floors where prisoners would sleep, a basement with toilets, and an attic. The sleeping arrangement was made of three-tiered bunks on each floor, each tier being thirty inches from the next one up. We would climb up like monkeys. I shared a bunk with five other inmates on the second tier. The floors were divided in four parts, each one called a *Stube*. Even though they had regular sanitary facilities, which was not the case at Auschwitz-Birkenau, the number of toilets in Auschwitz, about a dozen per block, were far from being sufficient for a thousand prisoners. There was running water there, but it was not good. The colour was dark and murky. I did not drink it. Because of our starvation diet, we only had bowel movements approximately once or twice a month. The stools were hard as sticks and we would have to break them up with our hands. When I think about it, I find it hard to voice this because I feel embarrassed.

There was a man who looked after the toilets. He had a wonderful job. He was called the *Scheißmeister* (Shit master). Different fellows took on that task. Sometimes it was a Jewish fellow, sometimes it was a Catholic or a Protestant. Everybody wanted to be a *Scheißmeister*. He was there in the block with a helper to clean the toilets, wash the concrete floor, and that was it. There were approximately twelve toilets in the basement, with six on one side and six on the other. I don't remember the exact numbers. The *Scheißmeister* managed the use of them by organizing the line of people. A Polish one in my block used to smile all the time and would say, "I can only take twelve persons at one time." It was a great job to be a *Scheißmeister*. He didn't have to go anywhere else. He only had to make sure that the toilets were cleaned. Of course, with inmates that had dysentery he had a bit more work to do. What was good about the job was that, in bad weather, he did not have to go outside to work.

Also nobody was beating him or standing over him with a gun. He was there as if he was hidden.

It was from Auschwitz, which was the main camp that they drew contingents of workers to go to different working places. They would send us sometimes to work on farms near the Buna concentration camp. In Buna, where I stayed at various times, the prisoners were not only Jews but also non-Jews. All nationalities and religions were mixed together. It is documented that many died from starvation, mistreatment, and execution in this camp. In the spring, we worked for about a month on farms near there during the planting season. I could see that in the camp there was construction going on. It did not take them long to build new barracks.

On a farm not far from Buna, the Germans kept their horses. A group of us was sent to work there and the Germans used to come and look at the horses. We had to brush the animals and make them shiny and spotless. We even had to wash the horses' feet. One day a German told me, "I am coming tomorrow, and if you don't clean the horses you will be dead." These horses were used in the fields for plowing, and we had to feed them in the morning and at the end of our workday. For that purpose they gave us bags of oats and buckets of thick black molasses from which we had to make a mixture with our hands. I tasted the mixture and discovered that it was sweet. We decided to eat some. We would chew the oats and spit out the shells. We must have eaten more oats than the horses. Had we been caught doing this we would surely have been shot. My God, with our starvation diet we were at least able to have a little bit more, but we only worked there for about a month.

Even with this little extra in my diet I still did not know if I could survive. To get more food, another way was found when we were sent to other fields to do farm work. We would pilfer potatoes and cabbage from the harvest. However, we could not pass the guards at the gate with this produce in our pockets. It would have spelt death for us. What saved us were nails we found on the ground and flattened with two rocks to make them like a knife that we kept in our coat pocket. We used these makeshift knives to slice the potatoes and the cabbage that we then put in our shoes in order not to get caught. We brought these vegetables back to the barracks to eat them. The problem was that we were always tormented by real hunger.

After Buna we went back to Auschwitz and from there to Auschwitz-Birkenau again, where we worked with airplanes. It was a site where they dismantled airplanes that had been shot down. Approximately twelve hundred of us were billeted to work there for a while. There were many Russian soldiers among the workers. These planes came on railways and had to be put on platforms and brought into a big long building, a sort of barracks, for the dismantling. We would break them apart using pliers and hammers and then put the salvageable parts in boxes. It was hard work. In the barracks where we were taking the planes apart we discovered that the Russians would make rings out of copper pipes that were extracted from the fuselage. That gave us an idea.

We could make spoons with pieces of aluminum from the planes. They were not great spoons, but they could pick up food. A couple of inmates would stand guard at the door to watch and inform us if they saw any soldiers coming. These makeshift spoons were an important commodity in the camp because we needed them to eat our food; they were also used for bartering in the black market economy of the *Lager*. What helped me survive was that I was strong and big for my age and I never got sick. I don't know from where I got all this energy. The other prisoners in my block used to call me *Liot Cheek* ("Pilot" in the Russian language). I could lift big barrels without any problem. However, I was not able to brush my teeth in all the years I was in the camps. We also ate anything that could be eatable. In some places, people were so thirsty that they drank their urine. I did it once.

Lice were a big problem. Apart from making our lives miserable from the itching, we had to try to get rid of them. The Germans, being aware of the problem, sometimes gave us a kind of powder that we would rub over our skin. Other times we would pick them and crushed them with our nails. Another way was to scrape some off our shirts, throw them on the concrete floor and take our wooden shoes to pound and kill the little pests. The lice were also on the blankets they gave us. We would have to take the blankets and, with our wooden shoes, knock them together on each side to kill the lice. The blankets had taken on the colour of black and red polka dots from the killing of these bugs.

In spite of my relatively good health in Auschwitz, I had to go to the hospital (also called the infirmary) when the bullet of a gun grazed my neck. A soldier was killing inmates at random. I felt the blood running, took my jacket off to stop the flow and walked for a while. Then I decided to go and have it checked by the doctors at the hospital. When I entered the building, I didn't know that there was nothing serious in there. They took a look at my wound and they wanted to put me asleep, but I would not let them do it. I fought the doctors, yelling and screaming. They even tried to cover my mouth with a mask. I pushed it away. Then I thought maybe God or an angel was on my side. I don't know. I told them that my wound was not a big thing. They finally let me have my way and they did not do much for that wound except patch it up. The scar is still noticeable today. However, they became aware that the inside of one of my hands was infected with pus. It had happened as a result of breaking stones with a hammer. They cut the skin with scissors, cleaned it and bandaged it. When this was done I was kept in the hospital to work.

I stayed in the hospital for maybe a week. I don't remember exactly how long. The sick were placed into a *Stube*, a part of the building with a big open space that had little narrow beds set up in three tiers. I slept on the second tier. Each bed was separate and measured twenty-five or thirty inches wide and had a little mattress and a little pillow. I never saw the linen being washed. Persons were laying there close to one another. Approximately two or three hundred people lay in beds there. There was no such a thing as a real nurse. What was called a nurse was a fellow like me walking around who they decided was well enough to care for the sick. All we could give them was a glass of water.

There was another big room in which they would take the ones that needed an operation. A glass window in the door allowed us to see what was going on in there. They were cutting bodies. I supposed they were doctors. I really don't know. But to us they seemed like butchers, even though they were nice young men. The Germans did not bother the sick. Sometimes they would yell at them, but not as loud as outside of the hospital. Many of the poor souls just lay in their beds until they died. Many died in the operation room as well. When prisoners passed away, we had to take them, put them on a stretcher and then carry them outside. We were maybe six or seven, or even ten doing this job. Among all the bodies we moved, there were not only Jews but also Catholics and Protestants from different nationalities. We recognized the Catholics by the crosses they wore. In the hospital I knew a few sick people that came from my town and, unfortunately, some died there.

When I left the hospital, they gave me bandages to

wrap up my hand and then they sent me to bricklaying school. The Germans trained many of us to be brick-layers. The training school was located at the Auschwitz concentration camp about two miles away from Auschwitz-Birkenau, in a building called Block 7A. This block had two storeys to house prisoners. The training school was in the attic. We were taught to build walls as if we were making buildings. We had to learn how to lay the bricks one on top of the other and make sure they would not fall apart. They gave us special trowels for this work that we had to learn. The walls must have been about three or four feet tall. Then we would take them apart and other fellows would build them up again. I did not stay very long at that training school.

Once, in Auschwitz-Birkenau, they closed up the barracks and nobody could get out. It might have been because there was an epidemic. They said there was a kind of sickness in the camp. I didn't understand what it was at that time, so I don't know what went on. One night while locked in, I dreamt about my grandparents. My grandfather touched my head and said, "You will be fine." In the camps I would also dream about my parents, my brothers, my sisters and my cousins. I still have those dreams today, as well as many nightmares. Sometimes these dreams are so real: I am jumping around and they are happy to see me. It does not matter how much I will talk about my experience; only those who were there can know that the deep scar, with which we were left, can never heal.

As part of Auschwitz-Birkenau, there was a group of about two dozen barracks separated from the rest by barbed wires. In these barracks there were whole families of Roma (Gypsy) prisoners—men, women and children. They never came to work with the rest of the inmates of the camp. We could see them across the barbed wire and they could see us. They came close to the wire and shook their fist at us, saying, "All you Jews are going to die!" They really meant all the prisoners on our side. The children would even throw small stones at us across the fence. One morning at *Appel* (roll call), when we were going to work, there was nobody on the other side of the fence. They had disappeared. A Polish *Kapo* told us that they had all been sent to the gas chambers.

In Auschwitz the violence of the Nazis was endemic. Once I saw two German soldiers beat a fellow to death at nightfall behind our block. The prisoner was screaming. In those situations we had to pretend not to see, because if caught just looking or saying something, we would be next, and this created great fear in us. The man died and other fellows told me that his body had been cut in half with the sticks used by his assailants. His body must have been so fragile that the beatings broke it completely apart. Others even told us that the man had been dragged across the sidewalk leaving a trail of blood and that they had been required to wash it away. The German soldiers were ruthless bullies. They took pleasure in being barbaric. It was sadism on their part. I don't know how to express the evil of such actions.

As long as I live, I will never forget another episode in which the Germans intended to dehumanize and victimize us. They made two thousand prisoners from two barracks go out completely naked except for their wooden shoes on a very cold late February night. We were so cold that we were rubbing ourselves against each other to try to keep warm. We were freezing, shivering. They then made us run a mile in powdery snow, at a temperature of at least five degrees below zero, before letting us go back into our barracks. Once back there, we shivered the whole night. They would shoot those who had fallen down. It was another way of getting rid of those who had become frail. Every night they would do this with a new set of barracks. I don't know how I survived. A couple of friends from my town and some Russian soldiers from my barracks died this way. Another way of eliminating those who were weak was to take a group of prisoners on a cold day and order them to lie down then stand up again, repeatedly, in a very quick manner for about an hour. Those who were not fast enough to do this were beaten to death with sticks. Often when I go to bed at night, these memories come to my mind and I feel like screaming "Why?"

One day they took a group of us from Auschwitz-

Birkenau or Buna to work on a farm. There was one Polish prisoner, four or five Russian prisoners and myself. They gave us big scythes for cutting hay. We were standing far across from each other in a straight line and a German was watching us. We had to cut the hay for a mile. One of the Russians was not well. Because we would have to do the work lined up together, he was not able to follow us in the line. The German came and asked him why he was behind. Another fellow told the German that the man was not feeling well—he had a bad stomach or something—making an excuse for him. I could see myself the illness in the face of that Russian fellow. The German came over and hit him a couple of times. The man was standing straight and did not move. The German continued beating him, just like one would strike a pole. I yelled out to him in Russian, "Fall down!" He would not do what I was telling him. The German took out his revolver and shot him right between the eyes. To me that was terribly brutal.

There was one Sunday in Auschwitz-Birkenau I will never forget. A couple hundred feet from me, I saw a fellow. I looked at him and told myself it could not be the person I was thinking of. He was a big, strong, chubby fellow like me and he looked familiar. He also was looking at me, and suddenly he yelled out my name, "Fischel." I said to myself, "Who is going to call me by my first name in here?" In the camps, they only used our number to address us. I finally recognized him and said,

"Cola?" He flew toward me and held me in his arms. He was a childhood friend who lived in a Christian Baptist village about two miles from mine and with whom I had gone to school. I started to cry and I asked him, "Cola, how come you are here? You are a Christian and I am a Jew. Why would they bother you?" He said, "First they took the Jews, and then they came after us." He was crying and shaking. I wanted to know what had happened to him. So I said, "Tell me, tell me, I want to know."

He told me that the Germans came to his village. There was a couple of dozen of them with trucks and they knocked on the door of his house. His father came out and they said to him that they wanted the cattle. It was an area where there were a lot of cattle. His father agreed that they could take a few, but not all of them. Hearing this, one of the Germans took a revolver and shot his father on the steps of his house. His mother got so hysterical that she grabbed a pitchfork and threw it at them. As a result, they took his mother and hanged her on a tree with her head down and her hands tied. They then made a bonfire and burned her. That was the way she died. I wanted to know what had happened to his two sisters, who were gorgeous-looking girls. He told me they had been raped by the soldiers and then shot.

I also wanted to find out about Cola's younger brother. He recalled the times when we used to go and play together. He then told me that the boy had been shot when both of them were close to the woods. He personally was not willing to run away and was captured alive. Finally I asked, "What happened to the town?" I learned from him that his town was all gone and, of the two hundred or so people who had made their home there, nobody was left. The Germans burnt the whole place, including the little Baptist church. Many of the people were shot dead and others were taken away. Cola indicated that it took ten days for him to be brought to Auschwitz in a freight car, although never knowing where he was going.

He then told me that, for the last two weeks he didn't like the work he was doing with steel. I said, "Why don't you join our group?" So he asked the *Kapo*, who was a Polish fellow, if he could leave and work with another group. The *Kapo* agreed. So he became part of my group, comprised of two hundred or two hundred and fifty men working on farms. The next day we got up early in the morning, at about five o'clock, for a three hours' walk to farms. We had to walk fast. We arrived at a farm where there was a big empty house with a well and a trough. Many farms in that part of Europe had big wells made of cement all around, with a trough beside them where they would bring the horses to drink. Once there, the Germans divided us for different jobs to be done. Twenty had to go there, and thirty to another place, and six somewhere else and so on.

For some reason, they kept Cola back. They didn't

like him, because they were already hitting him with a stick when we were walking in the morning. I think it was because he had freckles. I was maybe four or five hundred feet away from him, but there were people working closer to where he was. We knew each other and wanted to know what was happening to Cola there. Those who were near indicated that they didn't know. All of a sudden he was screaming and crying. The other fellows told me that the Germans had taken off his clothes and put him in the trough. They then took brushes, maybe steel brushes, and scratched all his body, even his face, possibly to take off his freckles. After awhile Cola was quiet. We did not hear him scream any more. I called out to the other fellows, "Any news?" Being far away from each other, those closer to the soldiers were afraid to talk too loud. With one of his hands, a fellow looked at me and made a sign indicating that Cola was dead.

Some of the workers saw his body all bloodied in the trough. They had to take him out of it. Prisoners made a stretcher with a piece of cloth and two sticks found at the house, and carried the body for the three hours it took to get back to the camp. My friend Cola was then burned and that was the last of him. From his village maybe a few were able to run away from the Germans but, so far as I know, he was the only one that had survived until he was tortured and murdered on that farm. Living under the Nazis was terribly disturbing; when they were not killing prisoners they were beating them all the time for nothing and would laugh, showing that they were superior to them. Taking pleasure in inflicting pain on people can only be a very sadistic way of being.

Those who tried to escape Auschwitz-Birkenau were shot and the Germans brought the bodies in the square for all to see. They used two-by-four planks of wood and with two pieces made an angle that would make these planks stand up. They had hooks on these contraptions with which they hung their bloody bodies by their clothes, with a sign that said SEE WHAT HAPPENS WHEN YOU TRY TO ESCAPE? The bodies were set up at the gates of the camp so people could see them. It may be hard to imagine, but one hundred thousand prisoners would pass by the gates on their way back and forth from work, starting at six o'clock in the morning, and they were ordered to look at those bodies when the Germans would yell to turn their heads toward them.

In other ways, if they caught somebody doing something with which they did not agree, or trying to escape, they would assemble ten or twelve of such victims and hang them on a rope attached to a scaffold. Thousands of prisoners in the barracks would have to come out and watch this. A German officer would come and, in a very loud voice, read out all the bad deeds that these people had done and accuse them of being traitors to the Reich. Then a sort of platform, on which the prisoners rested their feet, was pulled out from under them so that they would die from hanging. We had to stay there and witness all of this. I saw many ways how they murdered people. They even took pictures of these killings. All the pictures of the horrors in the camps and outside the camps, as many as a thousand of them, were taken by the Nazis themselves. Some of the soldiers would go with their photographs to higher-ranking officers and claim medals or more pay. I believe that they were one hundred per cent sure that they would conquer the world.

One of the very difficult experiences of life in those camps was the early morning rise at five and standing in line at *Appel* for an hour in all kinds of weather while they counted us. Prisoners were ordered to take out the bodies of those who had died overnight in the barracks and put them in front of us. The Germans counted them too. Other prisoners came with carts to take these bodies away to be burnt in the crematoriums. We also had to do *Appel* at noon and again when we came back from work in the evening.

Every day when we went to work people died at the work sites or along the way. There were always two, five, ten or twenty prisoners dying or dead around us. Again at the gates entering back into the camps, the Germans would count those who were alive and those who had died.

The selections in the camps were another example of terrifying and atrocious actions taken by the Nazis. I personally witnessed one or two selections. My memory is not too clear about two, but it was either at Auschwitz or Auschwitz-Birkenau, or both. Thousands of prisoners went to work around six o'clock in the morning and came back at about seven or eight o'clock in the evening. There was a place by the gates of the camps, a sort of platform that measured approximately a hundred and fifty by three hundred feet. When the prisoners passed near the gates, the Germans chose hundreds of them whose looks did not please them, were too skinny, or walked in a worn-out fashion. They made them take off their clothes. German soldiers would sit on two sides of the platform. The chosen prisoners had to hold their clothes up in the air with their hands and walk a hundred feet along the platform in front of these official observers. We had no idea who these Nazi officials were. They could have been doctors, for all I know. What these soldiers did was watch the men pass naked in front of them. They looked at their bones and determined their state of health. Then they would select a few, or as many as fifty prisoners, depending on their condition. They would then direct them to go to the left. Those selected were condemned to the gas chambers.

Persons like that were called *Muselmann* because they were only skin and bones, the skin holding the bones together. The use of the term *Muselmann* was a death camp slang word mostly found in Auschwitz for prisoners on the edge of death and showing symptoms of weakness and physical exhaustion. The soldiers had also different names for different groups of people. An example of this type of language was the word *Schweine* (swine) for English prisoners. Unfortunately, many inmates of the camps had to watch these selection processes taking place in front of them. It was for them an extremely stressful experience, for they did not know if their turn would come up or if they would be the next chosen ones. On their way to the gas chambers, the poor souls who had been selected were accompanied to their fate by a group of musicians. Music was an integral part of the concentration camp experience, whether the music was on command, for accompaniment, or staged performances. Among the inmates professional musicians had skills that the Germans valued because they enjoyed music. For instance, there was always music accompanying prisoners marching in and out of the camps. Musicians played marches so the prisoners could more easily keep in step with each other. In the case of a selection, music was perhaps just another attempt at deception. When the prisoners who had not been chosen went back to their barracks, they used to talk about what had happened to this fellow and that fellow. I knew some of them, but I have forgotten their names today.

One incident that remains in my mind to this day happened in Auschwitz-Birkenau, near our barracks. A group of us watched a truck delivering a load of bread to the camp. A couple of loaves had fallen off from the truck near where we were. We immediately ran to pick them up and shared pieces of the bread between us. Unfortunately we were seen by a German soldier who asked us why we had not put the loaves back on the truck. We had no answers for him and he made note of our numbers. In the camps we had no names, only numbers.

A few days later, this soldier came to the barracks and called our numbers. There were eight or ten of us. He ordered us to follow him to the gates of the camp. When we arrived, there were more German soldiers waiting for us. We were informed that we would each receive twenty-five lashes for what we did with the loaves of bread. They ordered us to stand up and then bend face down on a plank of wood that looked somewhat like a table but was a bit higher. They tied our hands, and the way our bodies were set up meant we could not move our feet. Some Germans started to lash my companions, who were screaming and yelling in pain. Each prisoner had to count the lashes, and if he didn't count the right number, the lashes would start all over again. I could see their flesh turn blue. Finally my turn arrived and a soldier did the same to me. He started to give me the same treatment as the others when suddenly, after the tenth lash, which felt like fire coming out of my eyes, I started laughing out loud and I could not stop laughing, even when I thought the blood was coming out of me. To this day I don't know what possessed me to react that way, but it stunned the soldier so much that he stopped and we were all sent back to our barracks. Even there I continued laughing, as if I was a madman. After receiving these lashings, we were not able to sit down for a whole week.

The next morning, I spotted blood in my urine. This concerned me because I thought that I was dying, and I had to go to work. Hearing about the blood and my concern that I would not live very long, a French inmate sleeping next to me said that he wanted to see my urine and check it out for me. I thought he was joking around. When we went to work he found a bottle and told me to pee in it. I did what he said and he went away with the bottle of pee. When he came back, I asked him what he did with it. He answered that he had heated it up to boil it. I said, "Are you a doctor? You are not a doctor, you are a farmer." He looked at me and smiled and said that I would live. He explained to me that a vessel had burst near my kidneys as a result of the beating. Apparently the vessel was closing. A week later the blood was almost all gone. There was only a little bit left. I asked him how he got into the camp, knowing that professionals were not thought of as useful to the Nazis. He had said that he was a farmer. In fact he was a doctor in his thirties, a very nice man with a dark complexion. He forbade me to address him as doctor or even tell anyone about his real profession. I will never forget him. When a male was under the age of eighteen or over the age of forty-five, he had no chance to live, but in between those ages and with the appearance of good health, the Germans would put him to work. But for the work he had to do he became a slave, which was no more than a beast of burden.

On another day near Auschwitz-Birkenau, I was working in the fields clearing bushes. I happened to see a dead man in a little brook which was part of some wetlands. I noticed that he had a pair of good boots on his feet. The top of one of my own shoes was torn. So I decided to take his boots in exchange for my shoes, since he was dead anyway. A German soldier saw this and started yelling at me. The soldiers were always yelling at us and beating us. However, I was able to keep the boots for a while. Maybe a couple of weeks later, they gave me new shoes. When they gave us new wooden clogs they would beat us, saying that we were sabotaging the government. That was the end of wearing my boots.

In these places, we were not all Jews. We were only twenty-five per cent of the working population. The prisoners came from all the conquered territories. A large number of Russian inmates were soldiers. When the Germans were screaming at us, many non-Jews did not understand what was being said because they did not know the language. Jews would often explain to non-Jews some of the things that were being said because the Yiddish language they spoke had words that were close or similar to the German language. Of course the Jews could not understand everything, and would grasp words only if the Germans spoke slowly. Unfortunately, all of us without exceptions had to suffer the brutality of the Nazi regime. These Germans had lost their souls and the capacity to see us as human beings just like them.

In our barracks there was a Dutchman who slept on a bottom bunk. I slept on the second tier and a Russian inmate I was friendly with slept on the third tier. The man from Holland was extremely tall and very skinny. I had never seen such a tall man in my life. One day the Germans came and took him away because he was a *Muselmann*. Another prisoner took his place in the bunk. He wore the Star of David on his clothes and I asked him if he was Jewish. Speaking in perfect German, this man got very upset and yelled, "I am not a Jew." He wanted to beat me up. So I shouted to the Russian fellow above me, "Misha, Misha, look at this little bastard who is wearing the Star of David and says he is not Jewish." The Russian got mad at the fellow, took one of his wooden shoes and hit him on the head. The man fell in the corner of the barracks and started to cry, repeating that he was not a Jew. Unfortunately for this poor devil, the Germans had informed him that his great-grandfather was Jewish. I looked at him and felt bad. I did not say another word. After awhile, I did not see him anymore. I asked other prisoners about him and they told me he had been killed. This fellow's reaction illustrates the deep anti-Semitic feelings that Germans felt, even if they had Jewish ancestry themselves.

There was a particular job, for which the Germans took at least a thousand of us prisoners, to build a highway that was about two or three miles long. There were many soldiers there walking around and watching us. Our job consisted of using hammers to crush big rocks and break them into pieces to make small stones. If a prisoner stopped breaking the rocks because he was tired or hungry, the Germans would beat him. Some of the men were standing a couple of feet deep in the road with picks and shovels, removing the yellow sand and throwing it out on the side of the road. This sand was replaced with the crushed stones. Everything was muddy; the earth was soft because it was raining. Again, if we stopped for some reason or another, the Germans would look at us and hit us over the head with sticks, saying we had to build the road more quickly. A hundred prisoners or more died there.

With us was a group of British soldiers who had been kept in the camp for a period of about two weeks. I was told that there were two hundred of them, but I only saw twelve or fifteen soldiers. They did not wear the camp's striped clothes, only their soldiers' uniform on which was written ENGLAND. Some of them were around us while we were building that road, but I did not know what they were doing. A few of them decided to snare a rat or a rabbit. I don't remember which one it was. It was very cold when we were working on those roads. Fires were made in steel barrels for the Germans and workers to warm their hands. After the little animal was caught, one of the English soldiers stuck it at the end of a wire and cooked it in one of those barrels. When it was cooked he gave us a piece of its meat and we ate it. When you are hungry and tired from hard work, you eat anything. In fact, we ate everything that was eatable: grass, live frogs, and all kind of things that we thought could provide us with nourishment. The British soldiers were treated better than the Russian soldiers, who got the same treatment as the Jews. One day the British soldiers left and we never found out where they went.

A few days later, on that same working site, a German soldier was coming down the road in a small vehicle. Suddenly, his vehicle broke down. It was very rainy and there was a lot of mud. Drunk and screaming, he ordered a number of prisoners who were working on the highway to lift the vehicle and put it on a platform truck that came along. Unfortunately the prisoners were too weak and were not able to do the job. The soldier killed them all with his machine gun. He then ordered another set of prisoners to go at it again, threatening them that they would be killed like the others if they did not succeed. Fortunately for them, they were successful. I did not see what was happening, although I heard the bullets flying and saw all the dead bodies. There were always dead bodies around wherever I was.

We were always going back and forth Auschwitz, Auschwitz-Birkenau and Buna. We were moved around for different work details. We would make friends for an hour or two, a day or a week, and then these friends would either die or be sent to some other place. I was also shifted to different locations. And we never saw each other again.

In Auschwitz I saw Heinrich Himmler, the one who oversaw all the German concentration camps. We had been told in advance that he was coming to visit. We had to line up in front of our buildings, standing straight in rows of ten. He was sitting in an open car with two other soldiers with him. His car was going all around the camp slowly, at the speed of approximately six miles an hour. He was accompanied by a delegation from the Red Cross. However, it was obvious to me that the people from this organization did not want to know what was really happening and were willing to sanction any crime being committed in the camp.

In Auschwitz-Birkenau, I was told by other prisoners who worked around a particular area that there was a special barracks in which women inmates were doing a specific kind of job. These inmates were called the *Kanada Kommando*. The barracks was surrounded by barbed wires. There was also a similar barracks for men that were also part of the *Kanada Kommando*. Both buildings were small. The work was connected with the people who were sent directly from the trains to the gas chambers and told that they had to take showers after being transported to the camp. These chambers had been set up for gassing people and consisted of two rooms. In the first room, the people were directed to undress and hang their clothes neatly on hooks attached to the walls so that they would find them easily when they came out of the showers. Once naked, the people would enter the second room that was made to look like a large shower room which would hold many people. The door would then close behind them and the men of the *Kanada Kommando* picked up all the clothes to bring them to the barracks of the women from the *Kanada Kommando*. In the second room there were shower heads on the ceiling. But the showers heads were not for showering; no water ever came out of them. It was a killing gas instead, called Zyklon B. When the gas hit the floor, it went up again, choking the people and putting them to death. The children died first. Everyone was vomiting because of the gases' nauseating effect. It took about ten to fifteen minutes for the people to die.

When they received the clothes from the men's *Kommando,* the women *Kommando* had to sort them out, take them apart and set them in piles. The women would go through all sorts of clothing and objects as well as check every lining and seam. They often found gold, money, precious stones, and jewels that had been sewn in. They made piles with each kind of items they found: gold rings, money, shoes, glasses, artificial limbs, combs, toothbrushes and many other things. Persons brought precious things because, not knowing where they were going and thinking that perhaps they would never come back, they thought that these objects might be of help to overcome difficult situations.

The women *Kommando* were watched by German women at all times. God help any inmate caught taking some of the precious items. However, some of the workers did manage to snatch some. There was a whole black market in the camps where these valuables could be bartered for food or cigarettes. Cigarettes were a precious commodity. Cigarette butts that would be found in or outside the camp would sell for a spoonful of water. But it had to be for one draw only. When the draw was seen as too long, the prisoners started fighting with each other. There were also many German civilians working in the camps along with the Nazis to make sure everything went smoothly. They were often ready to provide what some prisoners wanted in exchange for some money or treasures. They were themselves corrupted. The girls would wear the jewels that had belonged to those who had been murdered.

We would see *Sonderkommandos* from time to time. The nature of their job was to dispose of corpses and burn them in the crematoriums after they had been gassed. Because they knew too much about the Nazis' methods of extermination, they were usually murdered after three months. A new crew of *Sonderkommandos* would then take over the work. A few of these men came to our barracks because they had changed jobs or had gotten sick. Normally they were kept apart from other prisoners and had their own barracks. It is unthinkable to build crematoriums in order to burn the bodies of murdered people. Auschwitz-Birkenau and Auschwitz were not the only camps doing this. After the war, we learned that there were many other "death camps" using similar methods.

In the camps where I was, we did not know each other very much and, even if we did, we survived differently. If I was two thousand feet away from someone, or on another street, my experience might have been different. Maybe I was not there when a certain event happened or I did not see it. We wore the same clothes and had stars or triangles identifying our religion or our nationality. There was a different star or triangle with its own colours and shape for every category of prisoners. The fact that we were so tired and were sleeping on hard wood made us retreat into ourselves. It does not matter how much a survivor will describe his experiences; all cannot be told. We wanted so much to survive that we would do anything to be able to stay alive. Some could not survive because of the appalling conditions of hard labour, brutality, starvation, and lice. I lost all my family and too many relatives in that godforsaken place.

The highest position for a man in each building full of prisoners was called a *Blockältester*. These men spoke the German language. Maybe they did not agree with the Nazis about something, and that is the reason why they were sent to concentration camps. They were inmates like everyone else but had a better job. The German soldiers would come and talk to them. I remember that, in Auschwitz, one of our *Blockältester* happened to be a decent man. I also saw another one, a tall blond fellow, who could not take what was going on. Apart from the Nazi soldiers, some men seemed to be intent in making life unbearable for the prisoners. These were inmates who were foremen and who had to help the *Kapos*. The brutality of some of them was unimaginable, and with them our survival was continuously at risk. After my experiences in the Auschwitz concentration camps, I had to go to new camps where the situation was as grim and survival as precarious.

CHAPTER FOUR

Similar Conditions in New Camps

*L*OCATED SOME TWENTY-ONE MILES *northwest of Berlin, the Sachsenhausen concentration camp incarcerated many types of prisoners from 1936 to 1945. It is known that in this camp there were killings by shooting, hanging and gassing. The construction of gas chambers and ovens in 1943 made it possible to kill larger numbers of prisoners. It had all the same characteristics as other death camps, with the means to dehumanize and murder. Hard labour was the order of the day. The work was done outside of the perimeter of the camp in nearby brickworks or for different companies such as Heinkel, a manufacturer of aircrafts. For the prisoners the condi-*

*tions were atrocious. A very large number of inmates
died there due to exhaustion, starvation, exposure,
abuse and lack of medical care.*

I did not see the whole of the Sachsenhausen camp
because they took us to barracks. I just remember when
they brought us there. It was early in the morning. We
were maybe a thousand prisoners, and they formed several working groups, such as fifty here, a hundred there,
and so on. The rest perhaps stayed in barracks, or in a
special place. I don't know where they kept them. We
stayed there only a couple of weeks. Our group, which
was called the *Leichenkommando* (bodies transport team
or corpses *Kommando*), had to go to four or five small
barracks where we had to bend down to get in. In each
barracks there was straw covering the ground. The straw
was littered with dead bodies of men and young boys. I
would guess about fifty of them in each barracks. They
had brought us there to clean all that up. The Germans
had wagons of an old-fashioned style like we see in the
old cowboy movies. They gave us rope. With this rope,
we bent down and tied the legs of the bodies. Then we
had to pull these bodies outside. The stench was so
strong that I can still smell it today. Once the bodies were
taken out, we placed them on the ground. We then
helped other prisoners pick up these bodies and throw
them in the wagons. We had to haul these wagons back
and forth by ourselves along the road. There were no

horses. Some prisoners were in front of them to pull, while others were in the back to push. We walked with these loads for about two thirds of a mile, arriving at a place where another group of people had dug pits. These pits were about six to eight feet deep, and from the wagons we dumped the bodies in them. In this camp I personally did not get beaten, but I had to suffer the Germans screaming at us all the time. At first we were supposed to sleep in those barracks, from which we had extracted the dead bodies, but during our two-week stay we slept outside huddled against each other. They had made some kind of tents with poles and canvas and the prisoners slept there, if sleep is what you can call it. Then orders came to transfer us to the Oranienburg concentration camp.

The Oranienburg concentration camp was built in 1933 soon after Hitler came to power. Although in separate towns, Sachsenhausen and Oranienburg are part of the same complex. Both are often referred to as the Sachsenhausen-Oranienburg concentration camps. Located near Berlin, the administration of all the Nazis' concentration camps was carried out at Oranienburg. Early on, the camp acquired a reputation for the harsh treatment of its prisoners.

When we were taken to the Oranienburg concentration camp, there were already more than a thousand prisoners there who were placed in airplane hangars. We joined them in these hangars. We stayed in there day and night. Some of the soldiers used to shoot and kill prisoners in front of everyone. Their reason was that some of those prisoners could not walk, were weak or were thought of as *Muselmänner*. We remained there for a few days without doing any work. My guess is that they did not know what to do with us. Then, from Oranienburg they brought us to the Dachau concentration camp.

Like Auschwitz, Dachau is a concentration camp that stands as a reminder of the immensity of the crimes committed by the Nazis during the Third Reich. Located near Munich, at some point it held two hundred thousand prisoners from thirty countries, and Jews made up a third of the population. More than two thousand clergy were imprisoned in that camp and many died. Because new transports were arriving all the time, the camp became constantly overcrowded and the conditions were beyond human dignity and resilience. The Germans resorted to mass executions, and inmates were dying of diseases at a fast rate. Toward the end, an epidemic of typhus overtook the camp, and life became even more endangered for all the prisoners.

We were in Dachau for maybe a week. They made us stay day and night sitting on the ground in the large square used for *Appel*. We had to relieve ourselves there. We did not work. In the barracks where we were supposed to sleep there were too many dead people, mountains of bodies really. They had not been able to burn them yet. We could not remove all of the bodies; it would have taken us a month. Prisoners of the camp must have had to do this work. They told us that as many as four or five thousands were burned every day. Probably being aware of losing the war, the Germans decided to take our group away to the Landsberg concentration camp.

The Landsberg concentration camp, or Lager, *was one of the sub-camps in the tight network of the Dachau complex of concentration camps located in the districts of Landsberg and Schongau in Bavaria. In these various camps, prisoners were brought in from Russia, Poland, France and other occupied territories. They were used as slave labourers. Some of them worked for large firms nearby serving the German war industry. Two of them are the Bavarian Waterworks and the DAG (Dynamit Aktien Gesellschaft).*

When a new order came to walk us to Landsberg, the Germans that accompanied us were old men in their sixties and seventies dressed in their uniforms. They were very brutal with us. To get to this camp, we started early in the morning and walked until the evening. They wanted us to walk fast. They also killed at least two hundred or more people on the way. Landsberg consisted of eleven camps with six to ten thousand men in each. There were between fifty to a hundred hovels in each camp. I was first assigned to camp seven and later to camp eleven. The hovels of the camps were underground holes, which were about eight feet deep and measured twenty by fifty feet. They had been dug in the ground with roofs made of lumber boards mounted like an upside down V over the holes. One can picture this like a series of little roofs sitting on the ground. To sleep, we had to go down steps and lie on straw, which covered the earth. There were no sanitary facilities. We had to relieve ourselves under the straw or in a corner of the hovel. We were living there like rats in atrocious conditions. It was winter and the snow covered the roofs. We would eat the snow. At least that snow was good for providing more fluids to our bodies.

We stayed in Landsberg a few months. Our work consisted of constructing buildings which they told us would be hangars to store airplanes. We had to climb scaffoldings carrying bags of cement, lumber, or whatever they needed for the construction. These heavy materials were set on our shoulders and the Germans would position themselves under us and beat our feet with sticks. This was meant to make us climb faster. It was sheer brutality. The scaffoldings were placed at an angle with the walls of the buildings. On top of the construction there was a flat surface in which they had inserted steel rods. Once up there we had to unload our materials on that surface near these rods. Other prisoners would pour cement between the rods. The work shifts went on day and night. If I worked at night, I had to sleep in the barracks during the day and vice versa. We could hear American planes flying and bombing the area not too far away. When the planes came over us, the Germans used to scream at us, "Lie down flat!" We were not permitted to stand up during the bombing. If we dared to get up without their permission we would be shot. Many prisoners died in Landsberg because they had become too weak to work. For every bag of cement that was carried up the scaffoldings there were ten dead inmates. They did not have any crematoriums in this camp and I could see the corpses lying on the ground all over the place. I can still picture this gruesome scene in my mind.

From Landsberg, all the inmates of the eleven *Lager* were ordered to follow the German Army to the Tyrolean Mountains on the border of Bavaria. Up the mountains went soldiers, trucks, all their war equipment, and thousands of prisoners. I knew at that time that the Germans were losing the war, but I was so exhausted and weak that I didn't know if I would survive until the end of the hostilities. It was a long death march and many got killed on the way up the mountains. Thousands died also on that march, which was ongoing day and night. We were so tired that we were sleepwalking. They kept us walking without practically any rest. When trucks or tanks would break down, they tied the prisoners to them to pull the vehicles. It was tough and it was cold. They gave us only two pieces of bread to eat a day. The water we drank came from the streams that we would see here and there along the road. When we found icicles that we could suck on, that was like a bit of heaven for us. At least we had water. Once I went down to a brook after seeing running water, but I was so shocked to see the many dead bodies in the stream that I turned away from it. These bodies were prisoners that had been shot by the soldiers and thrown off the road.

I almost died there. A couple of weeks more of these conditions, and I would not be here today. On this march we were used as shields to protect the Germans from the bomber planes. The American planes flew very low over us but did not bomb us because they could see the mass of civilian prisoners, recognizing them by their striped clothes. We yelled at them to bomb us. We didn't care if we died because we felt that we were dead anyway. We hoped that they would kill Germans and destroy their equipment. However, they flew away.

I was there in the mountains for about three weeks with the German soldiers. The soldiers in the tanks were shooting down the hills, and there was shooting coming up the hills, most likely from the American Army, although I did not know it at the time. At nighttime we could see and hear flashes coming from both sides.

Suddenly, one day at midnight, the German Army went away and left us there with all their equipment. At daybreak, we looked around and we could see a river at the foot of the mountains. In the river there was what appeared like little black ducks crossing. Soon we realized that they were men, and these men were part of the American Army coming up the mountains. They were running or crawling like snakes. Under every outcrop of rocks and behind every tree there was an American soldier coming toward us. They had to go up the hills. They were telling us that we were liberated, saying, "You are free, you are free." Not knowing the language, we could not understand what it meant. An American soldier ran into me and said, "I am a Jew from Chicago, but I can't stay." He spoke Yiddish and had to follow his company. When I was liberated, somebody came and told us that there were three or four thousand dead prisoners in the hills about three miles away. He also said that, seeing this ghastly scene, the American soldiers covered their eyes and were weeping. The smell was so strong that they could hardly believe the horror of what had happened. The Germans killed these prisoners, not wanting the Americans to get them. A week more, it might also have been my own fate. After all these years of seeing atrocities, experiencing cruelty and living with death every day, freedom had finally become reality.

I ask myself how I managed to survive life in the camps. I guess I was too young to understand. I used to walk every day to work and saw people dying. Every day, they would throw the dead bodies out of the barracks because of the smell. I didn't pay attention. I did not think. My mind was blanked out all the time. It was as if I didn't see it and I didn't think about it. I was like a zombie. I didn't even know the days of the week. I didn't keep track. I saw the brutality, watched the killing, felt the stench of the barracks and the smell of the burning bodies, which I can still smell today. I helped carry bodies and bury them. Thank God I was strong enough to do this kind of work. Some of the prisoners could not and the Germans would go over, shoot them and throw their bodies with the other dead ones. The survival instinct enabled me not to think and do whatever they asked me to do. Being young helped me. At forty or fifty, a person might be thinking differently. I would sleep beside a fellow that was my friend for a week. Next week he was dead or one of us was transferred elsewhere. Every day, there were new prisoners coming in and every day they took prisoners out to another place or because they had died. I blocked it out of my mind. We were treated like animals and, sadly, in a way, we became like animals.

CHAPTER FIVE

Liberation

AT LAST LIBERATION HAD come, approximately twenty miles from the town of Bad Tölz, on May 2, 1945. The Americans were very good to us. They had come with trucks because they could see that we were practically skeletons and they feared for our lives. They brought us to a hospital to be checked out. They said I weighed seventy-five pounds. Doctors and nurses took good care of us. We were dirty and our skin had suffered the effects of dehydration. They had to clean us. They washed our bodies with cotton batten dipped in hot water. Then they smeared us with oil. They treated us like their own.

Once we got well, we could go out of the hospital on

our own. Many of us would walk on the streets. We were free. We could move around. We stood by the highway watching the American Army trucks carrying supplies. In the trucks soldiers would wave at us. One truck carrying clusters of bananas stopped. There must have been fifty of us. A soldier threw bananas at us. He was an African-American soldier and I had never seen such a man before because there were none in the area where I lived. Also, I had never seen a banana in my life. None of us had, again because we came from an area where they did not grow this particular fruit. Being kind, a few soldiers came and gave us each a banana that was half yellow, half green in colour. We did not know how to eat it and we bit into the fruit like we would do with an apple that still had its peel. It was too hard. The soldiers who were watching us started to laugh. One of them came down from the truck and showed us how to peel the banana before eating it. It was our turn to laugh, finding ourselves stupid for not knowing what to do. Tasting it, we found its flesh soft and delicious. After a week or two, we became well enough and the hospital personnel sent us to Feldafing, near München (Munich).

Feldafing was a German Army base that had been taken over by the American Army. It was used to shelter the survivors and help them recuperate from their ordeal. Everything we needed was taken care of. However, at first they would not give us much to eat because many survivors had died from eating a lot of food too soon. For that reason the doctors decided to ration us. We wanted more anyway, and I would say that I would not mind dying if I had more food. They fed us Carnation Milk because they wanted us to gain weight quickly. The first week, we were given a can a day. The second week, we were allowed two cans a day. After awhile we could drink as much as we wanted. We liked it a lot and it did not take too long for our weight to come back.

In entering the base, we were registered. The Americans took our names, the towns we came from, our parents' names and those of our grandparents. I would ask people if they knew what happened to the members of my family, but received no answer. The Red Cross was also working with the American soldiers. They gave us a paper indicating that we had been liberated from Dachau. It applied to Jewish as well as non-Jewish people. Our names were published all around the world so that families of survivors in America or elsewhere could find their relatives. We could live at the base which became a DP (displaced persons) camp: eat, take showers, sleep in a good bed and go anywhere we wished. We were able to stay there until decisions were made about where we would go after the war. I lived there for almost a year. We were finally free. We were not in camps anymore.

During that time, we were foolish like teenagers because in the camps they stole our teenage years away.

There were some Jewish fellows in the forces with whom we could speak Yiddish. My God, we could not get over it. Also there were American Jews in the Forces with guns. We didn't know anything about that. We also learned some English words from the soldiers. They would shout to each other, "Let's go, Shut up, Fuck you." We picked up these words and would repeat them, not knowing what they meant. When the young women in the American Forces, beautiful girls I must say, would ask us if we knew a bit of English, we would say those few words we had learned. They would laugh and tell us that using that language was not nice.

One day, a representative from the Red Cross accompanied by an American soldier came to Feldafing and said that he had a letter for me. I said, "A letter? Maybe somebody is joking around. Who is going to write me a letter?" I didn't know anything about someone writing me a letter, but the man from the Red Cross meant it and said that he would give me the letter on the condition I would sign that I had received it. And I signed. People around me, boys and girls survivors, wanted to see what the letter was all about. I opened the letter and the first thing that was written was: "I am your mother's sister." The letter was from my Aunt Celia Silver, who was living in Newfoundland. She had seen my name in the paper as a survivor who was her sister's son from the village of Shershev. She gave the letter to the Red Cross, asking them to track me down. I was under the jurisdiction of the American Army. That was the reason for the American soldier escorting the man from the Red Cross.

I almost died reading what she wrote and made the remark, "No, I don't like this stupid whoever wrote this letter." I thought somebody wanted to adopt me. I didn't know for sure and I didn't know what to think. So someone else read it for me. I could not read the letter because I was crying. In the letter, this aunt asked if anybody else had survived beside me. A fellow offered to answer the letter for me. It had been written in Yiddish. Unfortunately I lost the letter in the years that followed.

About a month later, I got a second letter from this aunt, this time addressed to me directly at Feldafing. From my answer to the first letter, she now had my address. Someone said, "Philip, you have a letter in the box over there." So I went to the box to see the letter, and the stamp was from St. John's, Newfoundland. It was a beautiful seven-cent stamp. I opened the letter, and in it there was a twenty-dollar bill in American currency. Everybody said, "Oh my God, maybe she could be my aunt." I cried again and could not write. A fellow wrote back in my place.

A week later, I received a letter from Montreal, Canada. I opened the letter and it was from my mother's younger sister, my Aunt Freida Wilansky, who had also inserted a ten-dollar bill in the letter. I liked the money but did not believe the rest because I would not allow myself to believe it. I knew my mother had sisters and brothers and that she had corresponded with some of them, but I thought that most had been killed during the war.

Sometime after that, I received a letter which also contained a ten-dollar bill. The letter was from New York and the person wrote: "I am your father's younger sister." I knew that my father had a younger sister living in New York. Her name was Molly Block. However, I did not know where New York was. These relatives had left Europe either before I was born or when I was a young child. The story is that, when they left Europe before the war, my father's sister knew my mother's sisters and they corresponded with each other from the United States, Newfoundland and Canada. These countries were free from wartorn Europe. After awhile, a second letter came to me from this aunt in New York. There was again ten dollars in it and she wrote that I would be fine. That was a lot of money in 1945. Between the three of them, my aunts decided to bring me to Montreal, Canada.

Then a letter from Chicago arrived, and it was written by a cousin of mine, the daughter of my father's brother who had died in 1938. She wrote that she was my cousin and put a five-dollar bill in the letter. I can never forget this. I was laughing and crying at the same time.

Having decided to bring me to Canada in 1945, my Montreal aunt went to Ottawa, probably accompanied by a lawyer. She asked a Canadian Government official if Canada would accept me, but he refused. It is well-known today that the liberal government under Prime Minister Mackenzie King held an anti-Semitic policy. It was only in 1948 that Mackenzie King, needing more workers, decided to accept a small number of Jews in Canada, thinking that nobody would notice. The book, entitled *None Is Too Many. Canada and the Jews 1933-1948,* illustrates the thinking in the immigration department at that time.[6]

Because Canada would not let me in, my three aunts then agreed between themselves to bring me to Newfoundland, which at that time was not part of Canada. My New York aunt suggested to my aunt in Newfoundland that she should go to her government and see if they would let me in. Otherwise, they would try to bring me to the United States. So this aunt from Newfoundland went to see William Joseph Browne the Judge in the Magistrate's Court and asked him about letting me come. His answer was, "By all means, right away." Soon after, the judge went to my aunt's house to bring her the necessary papers and help her fill them out in order to allow me to come to Newfoundland. These papers were put in a special document and sent to the British Embassy in Paris. My whole life was finally about to change in spite of haunting memories. I had lost my whole family living in Europe: my parents, my five brothers and two sisters, my grandparents, my uncles and aunts, my many cousins, and lots of friends. Later on, I was to realize that from the thousands of Jews in Shershev, maybe only twenty or twenty-five had survived. All around the area of my home, thousands of families were lost and no names have been recorded. It is as if they never existed.

CHAPTER SIX

Rediscovering the Goodness in Human Nature

ONCE THE DECISION WAS made by my aunts that I would go to Newfoundland and was accepted there, two British soldiers came to Feldafing with a Jeep in order to pick me up, and I was told that I had to go to Paris to get my visa from the British Embassy located there. I did not want to go. I said, "What the hell are you taking me for?" They replied, "No, no, you are okay, you are fine. One of your aunts has indicated that you can go to Newfoundland." I said, "Newfoundland, where is that?" We got a map to look where Newfoundland was. I said, "Gee, it is not far from New York." I did not know any better because I had never seen maps before. I wasn't able to evaluate the distance between the two places. So I went with the soldiers to Paris and they checked me in the Hôtel de l'Étoile near the Champs-Élysées. There I had to wait for about six months. Then I obtained a passage on a boat. The boat left Le Havre, France, to go to St. Pierre and Miquelon, islands that belong to France and are located very near the Newfoundland coast. From St. Pierre and Miquelon, the boat was going to New York, and in New York my three aunts were supposed to meet me. But I was so seasick on the boat that I was not able to complete the journey. I had never seen a ship in my life, let alone the sea. My aunt must have found a way to correspond with the vessel and was told that I was very sick. So it was decided that, when the boat would stop in St. Pierre, they would let me off there.

After leaving me off in St. Pierre, I stayed in a hotel called Hôtel Robert for a week. They helped me recuperate, they fed me. Everybody used to come and see me there. Some of them had been fighters in the resistance and they came on the same boat as me. One of them was Max Brie, who had been on the boat too. Monsieur Robert, the hotel owner, was a very nice man; I will never forget him.

Everything had been arranged and paid for by my aunts: the hotel in Paris, the boat passage, and the hotel in St. Pierre. All three aunts shared in the expenses. After a week, I felt better again and my Newfoundland aunt sent a special plane, a seaplane, to St. Pierre in order to bring me to St. John's. I found out later that the pilot's name was Jim McLaughlin. That was in 1946. I am not sure, but I think it was something like the first week of August.

We landed on a small airport in St. John's. My aunt was there with many people, cousins, and Judge Browne. They welcomed me and gave me a plaque on which was written WELCOME. FROM NOW ON YOU ARE A NEW-FOUNDLANDER. Judge Browne said a few words, among which saying they would help me get settled. I looked at him and started to cry. I was so emotional that I blurted out, "I don't want anything. I just want to be a free man." I was not able to speak English at that time, but my family interpreted for me.

After that little ceremony, I went to my Aunt Celia and Uncle Isidore Silver's house, where I was going to live. Still, then, I didn't believe that she was my aunt. I knew my mother had sisters, but I did not know where they were or who they were. I thought they all had been killed like the rest of my family. I did not know that one of her sisters lived in Montreal and the other in Newfoundland. I knew that my father's sister lived in New York, but I did not know where. He actually had two sisters in New York, but one had died in 1938 and I remember my father being very sad when it happened. We knew about New York, Chicago and Montreal, but how to get there or cross the water was beyond us. We had no idea of what the sea or even the world looked like. I lived about one thousand miles from the sea. In those days, I did not even care. As children, what we only cared about was what was around us and that we saw each other. My Newfoundland aunt had a beautiful home, and as I looked on the walls I saw pictures of my family and cried a long time. My mother had sent them before the war. It is then that I realized that she really was my aunt.

The first weeks that I was in Newfoundland at my aunt and uncle's house, I used to help out in the store that they owned. This store was the largest jewellery store in St. John's. It was called Silver's Jewellery and it was comparable to the Birks jewellery store in Canada. At that time, I did not know what to do. They wanted me to go to school. I didn't want to go, so they hired a private teacher for me. For some strange reason, I did not want anything from anyone. I didn't want them to help me. I wanted to make it on my own, even if it was the hard way. That was my personality, and the hard way was heaven in Newfoundland compared to the hell I had gone through.

I cried a lot and tried to tell my aunt things that had happened to me. Hearing this, she cried also and said, "Oh my God, Philip is sick; I have to take him to the doctor." She thought I was disturbed and knew that I could not sleep at night. She pleaded, "What can I do for you?" I answered, "Nothing. I just want to be alone."

Unfortunately, they could not understand because nobody but survivors understood what had happened in the camps. My aunt would say, "Maybe your father, mother, brothers and sisters were able to hide somewhere and are still alive." That, in a way, made it worse for me.

I did not work long with my teacher and I wanted to move out of my aunt's house. I had cousins in Newfoundland related to my mother. All my relatives in North America had immigrated either before or after the First World War. These cousins from my mother's side used to say to me, "Our grandfather and your grandfather were brothers." I therefore had an extended family in this part of the world. I could not speak the English language, so I spoke with my aunt, uncle and cousins in Yiddish. My Aunt Celia's children, two girls and two boys, didn't speak Yiddish. They learned a bit of Yiddish from me and I learned a bit of English from them. I loved my newly found family and had fun with the children, Max, Cyril, Rosalie and Cynthia.

At one point I went to live with my cousin Ida Wilansky and her husband Herzel. They had five children whose names were Sam, Maurice, Douglas, Pearl and Sandra. I was particularly close to one of their sons, Maurice Wilansky and his wife Sonya. They lived in St. John's. He and his wife had three children: Graham, Melvin, and Dorothy. My cousin realized that something was bothering me and he wanted to know how he could help me. I said to him: "All of you are so kind and good to me and want to help me, but I want to make it on my own." He was already established with a clothing store called Wilansky and Sons. He indicated that he would help me out with what I would choose to do. I asked him, "How did those who came here before me start their business?" He answered, "At the beginning of the twentieth century, they would go around selling from door to door with a pack on their back. The first thing is to learn the language as you go along." With this advice, my cousin gave me all kinds of clothes and linen and told me, "Take whatever you can take with you and go by train to the town of Holyrood."

So it was in October 1946 that I became a peddler. On the advice of my cousin, I took the train to the town of Holyrood. There I went selling from door to door with a pack and two suitcases full of clothes: work pants, work shirts, socks, ladies' and children's fleece-lined bloomers, boys' pants, and various small articles, such as combs, handkerchiefs, and razor blades. They were the types of things that people wanted. I also had some linen to sell. After this first outing, I developed a routine of travelling by train to a town where I stayed for a day or two and walked around all the little places. Someone would give me a room to stay overnight. I would sell all my goods and go back to St. John's.

Right after the war, there weren't too many stores, and those in existence did not have many goods to sell. Actually, there was a shortage of merchandise, and anything that could be found was very inexpensive. The first week, I made five dollars, and the next, ten dollars. The following week, I made nothing, but I had not spent the money I made. In St. John's, I slept at my cousin's or my aunt's place. They would not take any money from me. When I offered they would laugh at me. However, I always paid back the merchandise my cousin gave me to sell. My aunt was not too happy when I stayed with my cousin, but I would go to her house as well, stay there, eat there and have fun with her children. I really loved all my young cousins. They were like my own. In a way, I was still a kid myself.

In my aunt's house there were bedrooms everywhere. They washed my clothes and did everything for me. Of course they had help in the house, a maid who was a very nice girl. During the Jewish holidays, I would come and help them with the preparations. They offered me all kinds of money, but I refused to take it. I would say, "You are going to ruin me. I don't want anything. I just want to go my way. Please understand me."

I went to many little towns to sell my goods. This is how I discovered my new country and its wonderful people. What struck me most was that people were so kind to me. I could not believe it. They would say, "Come in, come in, have a mug-up," which meant come into the house and have lunch with us. They would prepare a whole table of food and share their meal with me. In every house, they could not have done more for me. I learned English from them. Slowly I became able to speak the language and understand what people were saying. I was young, in my early twenties, and appreciated so much their kindness. They did not have very much, but they shared whatever they had. It was hard to comprehend the very sharp contrast that it offered from my years at the hands of the Nazis. When I would go to my room, I would often cry and didn't want anybody to hear me. I covered myself up. After awhile I would wash my face and join those who had offered me their hospitality by giving me lodging and sharing their meal with me. I craved so much for my family. I felt like they were my own brothers and sisters.

I went peddling to a place called Harbour Main. There was a lady who had a little store there, and I was able to sleep at her house for two nights. Her name was Ann Murphy. She was a very nice person. She gave me a bed, breakfast in the morning, and supper when I came back late at night. Most incredibly, she would not take any money from me. When I finished my rounds, I walked to Conception Harbour, which was not that far, and would come back to Harbour Main for the night. What was different from what I had known in Europe was that these villages were surrounded by the sea and the houses were all made of wood. And in those days, most of the roads were dirt roads; they were only paved as far as Bay Roberts.

Not too far from Harbour Main, maybe Chapel's Cove, I

got off the train with my pack and two suitcases. I started walking on the railroad tracks until I saw some houses. I left the tracks to go to the first house. There was a man carrying wood on his back who saw me. He asked me if I had any towels. I did not know what he meant, so I opened up my suitcases and he spotted the towels. He bought two sets of them and paid me. Of course, all the prices had been written down so I could show the customers.

On one of those days, it was after 6 o'clock in the evening and already dark. I decided I would stay overnight in a little town called Burnt Point. I saw a little store there, walked in with my pack and two suitcases and I said to the storekeeper with the little English I had learned, "Me stay overnight?" He asked me, "What do you do? Are you a peddler? Are you Jewish?" I said, "Yes." He told me, "You will stay in my house." He called his wife: "Mildred, we have a guest here." His name was Eli Handcock. They cooked trout for my supper. They gave me a nice room and a comfortable bed to sleep. Before I went to bed, he said to me, "God bless the Jews. There would be a thousand men outside standing and I have only one bed. Among these thousand, the Jew gets the bed. He is one of God's chosen people." And he got so excited that he did not know what to do for me. He bought everything that was in my pack. He then suggested that I go selling to stores instead of going to the public. After the war, they could not get many goods.

They had quotas to get a certain amount and that was it. However, my cousin Maurice Wilansky and others would supply me with goods and only charged me what they had to pay. They were very good to me.

People had very little at that time. They could not buy pants, for example. A dressmaker could make them, but imported, factory-made clothes took time to be available. For instance, work pants, green or brown, which stores would normally charge for a certain price, I would give to the customers for a few cents less. I made a little profit and that was good enough. So when they took a dozen of this and that, oh God, I made a few dollars. At that time it was a bit of money. I was happy; I thought I was getting rich.

On a day when I came back to St. John's to pick up more goods, my cousin told me to go to Clarenville. It was further away from St. John's than the other towns I had been to. The train got there at eleven o'clock in the evening. It was the month of October and it was very dark outside. When a train comes in, many people go to the station to meet friends or family on their arrival. I got off the train and saw a few children around. I wanted to know from them where I could stay overnight. But not knowing how to speak English too well, I made a sign that I needed a place to sleep by putting my two hands together on the side of my head and slightly tilted it. When I left St. John's, my cousin had written on a piece of paper, "Can you board me overnight?" With this paper,

I could show people what I needed. The children told me to leave the station and pointed to a house, which occasionally provided boarding for the night. It was a nice house not far from the water.

After knocking on the door, I looked for my piece of paper and could not find it. The lady opened the door and I was still looking for the paper. She said, "Yes, can I help you?" She did not get any answer, so she repeated her question. I did not know what to do. I almost started to cry. I could not find my paper and there were two or three children there, one of whom was a girl of about fourteen or fifteen. I wanted a room to board and finally said to the lady, "Me, sleep with you." She saw my pack and suitcases and realized that I could not speak English too well. However, she understood what I needed. She said, "Come in, come in." She made me something to eat and gave me a room to stay overnight. When I got up the next morning, she gave me breakfast. Her name was Mrs. Seaward. I tried to talk to her a little bit. I did not have any money on me, so I wanted to give her something, a handkerchief or a comb. She did not accept it and did not charge me for my stay. There were many children around there and they helped me carry my pack and suitcases from house to house. Mrs. Seaward insisted that, when I finished going around selling, I would come back and stay at her house again. So I stayed there two nights. Mrs. Seaward's husband worked on the railway. She had a daughter by the name of

Mildred and a married son who had two children. His name was Clayton. His children used to teach me English by making me repeat the names of the goods I was carrying around. When I moved to Nova Scotia in 1980, a member of her family called me. During my second day in Clarenville, a tall slim fellow came over to me and asked if I had men's socks. His name was Jim Noseworthy. The children around helped me open my suitcase and he picked up two pairs of socks which he bought from me. He then told me that he worked on ships. He also helped me learn some English words. Later on he became a policeman in St. John's and we ended up good friends.

After my two days in Clarenville, I walked to Shoal Harbour, where I went peddling to different houses and sold many things. It was not far away and there were houses all the way along. In those days, I was young and walking was nothing for me. From Shoal Harbour I went as far as Milton that day. When I arrived, it was dark and I saw a red barn. I slept in that barn overnight without anybody seeing me. Early in the morning, a lady came out of her house on her way to the barn. She noticed me near the barn. She yelled out to her husband, "Frank, Frank, there is a strange man around the barn!" He came out and saw that I was selling things. He was a very caring man. She also was kind. She invited me in the house and made breakfast for me. Their names were Clarice and Frank Adams. They owned a beautiful home and a gasoline station. She bought a few things from me. She called her mother and her brothers who also came over to the house and bought some of the goods I was selling. I will never forget them. Her mother bought a pair of black britches with leather on the knees for her eight- or nine-year-old son whose name was Maury. He is still alive, because I saw him years later. Mrs. Adams's father also purchased a few items.

I worked around the town selling and came back to stay with them that night. She was a very pretty lady and had such a good heart; she was a real human being. I must say that the whole family showed thoughtfulness toward me. Surprisingly to me, Mrs. Seaward was a relative of theirs. They would speak to each other on the phone, which at that time was a multiple-party line. While I was in that area for three days I sold quite a few of my goods. I had already made about twenty-five dollars. At that time it was a lot of money. However, the night I spent in the barn was difficult for me. I cried and nearly fell apart, thinking of my family and the friends with whom I went to school. Such a situation was to be repeated over and over again. For forty years I would not speak about what had happened to me. People knew I came from Europe, but that was all.

I left Milton, still having goods to sell in my luggage, and headed on foot for Lethbridge and Brooklyn. On the way to Lethbridge, a fellow gave me a lift with his horse and buggy. I sold some of my goods there and started out for Brooklyn. On the road to Brooklyn, another fellow with a horse and buggy picked me up. It was late when we arrived, but I walked around the village selling things. At one point I came to a house where the owner bought some children's clothes. He told me that it was too late to go selling and offered me to stay overnight at his home. His name was Phonse Stears. This type of generosity was to be found all over Newfoundland. The next day, a person gave me a lift in a pickup truck back to Clarenville for me to catch the train to St. John's.

On the following trip, I went to Port Blandford by train and arrived around midnight. The station master was curious and, seeing my pack and suitcases, wanted to know my line of work. He soon realized that I was a peddler because I was a very strong fellow able to carry those bags with no trouble at all. He gave me good advice, saying, "People will be up when you see smoke coming out of the chimneys." At seven in the morning, he left the station and soon returned to take me to his house to have breakfast. He was a real gentleman. His name was George Thomas. His wife was a teacher and a lovely person. They served me fried eggs, toast, and coffee. They were very smart. Knowing that Jewish people do not eat pork, they did not give me bacon. She taught me the English song *You Are My Sunshine*, drawing the sun with a crayon. She also taught me the song *Give Me Five Minutes More*, wanting me to understand the language better. After awhile, we became good friends. George had originally come from Hant's Harbour.

From Port Blandford I went to Charlottetown by boat across the bay. When I got there I walked into a store which was owned by two brothers, Les and Dan Spracklin. They bought some of my goods. Then they brought me to their house, gave me something to eat and let me stay overnight with them. I cannot say how considerate they were with me. It was overwhelming. While there, I realized that every little settlement had a wharf. Boats would ferry people back and forth to the different villages around. I finally left Charlottetown and went back to St. John's to restock. I stayed there for a few days to visit with the family and got ready to go back on the road.

With my new load of goods, I took the train further west, to Terra Nova. It was a place where many men worked in the woods for the Bowater Company and lodged in a camp. When I arrived, the station master wanted to know my name and I told him. He said to me, "Are you going to have a nap? I want to have a nap." I did not know what he meant, my English being still very limited. I saw him clean the table, put some kind of mattress on it, lie down and put a blanket over himself. I was sitting on a bench, watching him. A few minutes later I went to him and shook him a little. I said, "Me nap too." He fetched two blankets and settled me on a bench in the station. I made a pillow out of the first blanket and covered myself with the other. The station master's name was Tom King. Later that night, he used Morse code to connect with the trains, then left and told me he would be back in a few minutes. When he came back he brought me a bottle of very strong homemade beer. After drinking it, I slept very soundly that night and the station bench felt like a mattress. Over time we became good friends. He had children and would often bring me a sandwich. He took interest in me. He enjoyed teaching me English and correcting some of my mistakes. He was a very kind-hearted man.

Early the next morning, at about five or six o'clock, I went to the camp where the woodsmen were lodging, thinking I would sell a few of my goods. At that particular time, the men were preparing to leave and go to work. The foreman, whose name was Max Moss, told me that when the men would come out from the woods later on in the day, they would want to buy things from me. He said, "Look, I am going with them, and in the meantime you can take my bunk and sleep for a few hours." I went to his bunk and slept for a while. A bit later, I went back to sell to the few houses in the town and got back to the camp when the men returned. I sold them pants, clothes, even combs and razor blades. They cleaned me out. Max Moss was a very nice young man.

My next destination was Glovertown. On the train I brought a big trunk full of merchandise as well as my usual pack and two suitcases. The settlement of

Glovertown was about a couple of miles from the station. Taxis would drive back and forth the people that were either arriving or leaving. The taxi driver who picked me up with my trunk and my bags arranged for me to go to the town and check into a hotel. He happened to be the owner of the hotel, which was called Ackerman's. His name was Caleb Ackerman and his wife's name was Dorothy. When I arrived, the building was brand new and it was like a big boarding house. They told me that there had been a fire a couple of years earlier and it had burnt a good part of the town. People had built shacks with corrugated iron to shelter themselves until they rebuilt their homes. Construction of nice homes had started at the time I was there, but one could still see some of the shacks. I stayed there for ten days, walking around and selling not only in Glovertown but also in Traytown, Eastport and all around the area. All this time, Caleb and his wife fed me, lodged me and would not charge me for anything. Caleb would not even accept money for taxiing me back and forth to the railroad station. What was striking for me around those towns was seeing the boatloads of fish at the docks.

A few days later, I walked from Glovertown to Eastport and knocked at a door of a house. Lo and behold, who answers the door, but Max Moss from the working camp at Terra Nova. He was pleased to see me. He and his wife gave me lunch. She was a very sweet lady, and pretty I must say. They also had children. I was amazed by their generosity, and with time we became very good friends.

On another trip further on I arrived in Lewisporte by train with my trunk, my pack and my suitcases. The train stopped near a hotel which was called Manuel Hotel. I stepped out of the train; I went into this hotel and asked if I could stay overnight. The man agreed, and I wanted to know how much he charged. He looked at me and said, "What is your line of work?" I answered that I was a peddler. He said, "You stay here with me." I repeated, "How much do you charge?" He answered, "For you, there will be no charge." And he called his wife down. His name was Lance Pelley; he was the owner of the hotel. Every morning I went peddling my wares around from house to house. At the end of the day, this man bought whatever was left over in my suitcases because he also had a store. He took everything and paid me. I went out in the morning and walked for miles and would come back in the evening. The hotel owner had girls working for him, and when I would come in they would give me hugs. Being dinnertime, Mr. Pelley also would make sure that I ate with him and his wife at the same table. They even helped me with my English. When I left, taking the train going back to St. John's, my suitcases were empty. He also took two hundred dollars out of his pocket and wanted to give it to me. I would not take the money. I almost cried from happiness that these people were so generous with me.

He gave me a piece of paper on which was written his name, his phone number and his address. He had also written the words, "If you get sick or need anything, please call me and I will come and get you. And we will look after you. We love you people." He was an amazing person!

Then I found out that Mr. Pelley had a brother in Port Blandford. He called his brother and his mother and father and, sometime later on a Sunday, he flew me there so they could meet me. His brother, whose name was Burt Pelley, became another customer of mine. He was such a good man. Once I started to cry and he gave me a big hug. From then on I started to sell only to stores.

In those first few months of peddling my wares I had gone where the train could take me. I walked all around the different areas from house to house. I was trying to make a living, not get rich. Many people there who were fishermen were scratching out a meagre living. For what I sold I made sure that I only made a small profit, which I saved up.

On my second trip to Clarenville, I sold to small stores. They had everything, even food. I happened to go to a store called Stanley's, the owner being Philip Stanley. The kids used to call him Uncle Phil. His wife, Mrs. Stanley, was a very nice lady and invited me for lunch. They had two sons. She also told me that I should sell to stores instead of houses because it would be easier for me. She understood that going from door to door was hard work. She picked out some of my goods and bought them for her store.

One day after a big rain, my shoes became full of water. I sat down near a rock, took my socks off, washed them out, drained out the water and put them back on. I then ran with my baggage a mile or two and I could see the steam coming out of my shoes. I was really hard on myself, but it was my decision. Nobody was punishing me. I hardly had any money and I would not ask my relatives for some. I would not tell anybody about the previous part of my life. I used to sleep in barns and on railway station benches. I would cry, thinking about what had happened to me in Europe, but I did not want people to see me cry. When I met people I was always nice and would smile. I learned the language from them. After awhile, I got to know a lot of people, became successful, and was able to make a living.

Everywhere I went, I was well-received, and people such as Craig Giovannini and his family in the mining town of St. Lawrence boarded me in their hotel without ever charging me. I asked about renting a space for a little store there at Christmastime and they did not charge me a cent. Every evening they would kneel down to pray with all their children and say, "Hail Mary, full of grace, pray for us sinners and God bless Philip Riteman." Aubrey Farrell and his sister Ena, who had a store in that town, also bought my goods. I very much appreciated the consideration they offered me.

Once, a storekeeper shared with me something his mother had told him. She had said, "If you see a Jewish person that has to make a living and you buy from him, God gives you five times back." When people talked to me in that way, I did not know what to think because I was still a survivor who had experienced too much cruelty to believe in a different world view. However, the people of Newfoundland were the ones who helped me look at life in a different way.

In the winter months I did not go peddling too much because it was hard to travel. During that time, I would help out in my uncle's store. One day it was very icy on the sidewalks and there were many people in the store. My uncle told me in Yiddish to go and tell Marian, a head girl in the store, to take salt and sprinkle it on the sidewalk. So I said, "Marian, Marian, Uncle said to take salt and *shit* (the Yiddish word for sprinkle) it on the sidewalk." I did not know the English word for sprinkle. There were a few girls working in the store and they all started to laugh. In an instant, Marian grabbed me and pulled me into the office. She put her finger on her mouth, indicating to me that what I said was not a good thing to say. Then she showed me what the word meant by acting it out, slightly lifting her skirt. I was terribly embarrassed finding that out, but it was a lesson well learned.

The time came when I wanted to carry more goods with me. I had been a peddler for a while and I wanted to buy a van. I had saved a few hundred dollars, but it was not enough to make the purchase. My aunt and my cousin wanted to give me the money for the van. I took six hundred dollars from each one and assured them that I would give it back. They would always laugh at me when I would say that. They wanted so much to help me with anything I needed, so long as I was happy. And they never accepted that I pay back the loan.

With the van I went to a place called Bay de Verde. There was a store there called Quinlan Brothers. One of the owners, whose name was Pat Quinlan, bought some of the goods I was selling. It was late and I had to stay overnight. He took me to his father's house at Red Head Cove, where he was living as well because at that time he was still single. They had a big room and two beds. There was one bed for Pat and another one for me. During dinner that evening, they said that they had to go out in their boat and check their cod traps at four o'clock in the morning. They wanted me to go with them. I said, "Four o'clock, you have to be crazy, I am not going with you, It's too early and too dark." They were laughing at me. We went to bed and, at four o'clock in the morning, the father came into our room and said in a low voice, "Pat, it's time to wake up." Pat woke up, got out of bed, shook me and asked me again to go to with them. I refused. They came back at about ten o'clock. They told me they had a lot of fish. They made breakfast. We ate together and became very good friends. His brother

Morris was a schoolteacher in St. John's. Time and again I went selling to Pat's store. Later on he got married and built a new home. I stayed with them a couple of times. His wife's name was Marie. I knew the whole family very well and they were always very nice to me.

With the van I went to Old Perlican and sold to a store called George Hopkins Ltd. There I met a lady whose name was Freda. At that time she was single and a schoolteacher. Later on she married Weston Hopkins, the owner of the store, and they had a son and a daughter. She was the finest lady on the planet. She was so generous. She always bought my merchandise. I knew her children when they were little, their names being Fred and Pauline. After her husband Weston died, she had to run the business by herself. A lot of people came to her and wanted to sell their goods. She would say, "No, no, I want to buy from Philip." In her own words she talks of a very unique relationship that developed between us, an everlasting one, based on trust and respect. Years later, her son Fred married Pat Quinlan's niece. They lived in Pat Quinlan's father's house for a while before they built their own home. I went and spoke to the students in the school at Old Perlican a couple of years ago. Freda appreciated the fact that I have been telling my story for a number of years now. She wrote me a letter. The following excerpt describes her feelings:

"Philip! No words can describe your contribution to Education and the enlightenment of all these students to whom you have spoken in Canada and in the U.S.A. about the horrors of the Holocaust. As you continue to speak of the unspeakable I trust that you will not falter, but gain renewed strength."

Her daughter Pauline is a schoolteacher and has integrated my story in her academic program. To this day, Freda and I remain very good friends.

In January 1948, on a trip to Montreal to buy goods and to visit my aunt, I met Dorothy Smilestein, who was to become my wife. Her grandfather rented rooms to newcomers. He had rented rooms to a couple, both survivors like me. They had come to Canada in 1948. The woman was from Pruzhany, where my mother and my Montreal aunt came from. This aunt was called Freida Berger Wilansky. She had married Joe Wilansky, who had a business in Botwood, Newfoundland, and later started a business in Montreal. They had two children, a boy named Michael and a daughter named Esther. The woman survivor knew my Montreal aunt from the old country. She also had been in the Pruzhany ghetto. She got married right after the war to a Jewish man from Latvia. I knew her because she was a displaced person and we were both in Feldafing. She married there before coming to Canada. I had lost track of her because I went to Newfoundland in 1946. Her name was Esther. My aunt wanted to go and visit her and asked me to go along. When we arrived, Dorothy was there with her mother, visiting also. They had become friends with this young couple. At that time my English was not too bad and I asked Dorothy if she could introduce me to some of her friends. She did not follow through. Maybe she wanted to keep me for herself. In any case, I called her up a couple of days later and asked her if she would like to go to a movie with me. She agreed and we went to the movies together. That was the beginning of our courtship. We married two years later. It was 1950 and the marriage took place in Montreal. In the meantime, Newfoundland had become part of Canada in 1949.

I was always in touch with my New York aunt, Molly, and her husband, Chaim Block. I used to write her often and talk to her and her family on the phone. She had two married daughters, Rose and Fay, a son, Larry, who was single at that time, and twin girls, Gladys and Thelma, who were also single. I called her to tell her that I was engaged and was going to be married. I told her that I would love for her to come to my wedding. Until that time I had never met my aunt in person. I was delighted that she could come and, when I saw her, I realized that she bore a strong resemblance to my father's other sisters. She was a very attractive lady. To this day, I remain very close with her children, my American cousins, who are about my age. My heart is always full of love for them. I had other cousins in

Chicago, the children of my father's brother, Lewis Riteman. One of them came to my wedding. Unfortunately, the connection with them was not as strong as with my other cousins, who are like sisters and brothers to me. However, I also have cousins in different parts of the world. My paternal grandfather Riteman had five brothers and two sisters and my maternal grandfather Berger had six brothers and three sisters. Some of those aunts and uncles had spread out away from Europe in countries such as the United States, Canada, Argentina, Israel and Australia. The name Riteman has a different spelling in some of those families. I am fortunate to have had visits with these cousins over the years.

After our wedding, Dorothy came to Newfoundland. We raised two sons, both finishing all their schooling and higher education there. We enjoyed a very rich life with family and community. Our house was always open to friends. We took pleasure in the company of many soldiers from the Fort Pepperell American Army base in St. John's. We are still in contact with some of them today. I can never forget that it was the Americans that had liberated me in the Tyrolean Mountains.

When Dorothy first arrived in Newfoundland, she wanted to correct my English. Once, when I was selling something to a customer, she started to correct what I was saying. That person countered, "Don't correct Philly because we like the way he speaks." While I was on the road, my wife was very involved with the Jewish community and also volunteered in numerous non-Jewish charitable organizations.

I eventually got out of the clothing business to go into the selling of floors, wall covering, and carpets. I had a new building constructed in St. John's and it was called Riteman's Limited. I used it as an import business from Europe and my territory was all of Atlantic Canada. When my company became successful, I needed the expertise of a lawyer. I sought the services of the law office of Tommy Williams and Harry Cummings. Their advice was very much appreciated and they hardly ever charged me for a lot of work they did on my behalf. They always showed me consideration and respect. When these men found out that I was a survivor from the concentration camps, they both came and gave me a big hug accompanied with tears. They said that if I needed anything they would help me.

Life was good in this beautiful Island. However, my business could only prosper if I had close access to a container port, which Newfoundland did not have. This was the reason why I left my beloved Newfoundland in 1980 and came to Halifax, Nova Scotia. In this new province, I had to cope with some of the ups and downs of the economy, but as things got better I kept going. Around the year 2000, when I was in my mid-seventies, I decided to wind down my whole enterprise and it took me a couple years to close all my accounts.

There are so many more people and so many places in

Newfoundland and Labrador that I would want to mention, but I cannot name them all. I would have to write another book. I travelled all over the Island. There are very few settlements where I did not go. I went by boat to remote islands and outports. The people were most hospitable and considerate. They would ask me where I came from and called me the Jew with the curly hair. When later they learned that my name was Philip, they would hug me and say that I was part of God's chosen people. In my heart I say God bless them all for welcoming me, making me one of their own and recognizing me as a human being. Newfoundland will always be a very special place that helped me survive my heavy emotional burden. People did not know my life story. They only found out later. To this day, I cannot forget all the kind-heartedness shown to me by the Newfoundlanders. I feel as if all of them are my brothers and sisters. It is with them that I rediscovered the goodness in human beings.

CHAPTER SEVEN

Telling the Story to Educate

STARTING IN THE 1960s, there have been a number of persons worldwide who have tried to deny that the Holocaust ever took place. In Canada in the early 1980s there was the well-known case of James Keegstra, a high school teacher in Eckville, Alberta, who was teaching his students hateful things about Jewish people and saying that the Holocaust was a myth created by Jews to gain sympathy. He was convicted of hate speech. The case made its way as far up as the Supreme Court of Canada, which upheld the conviction.

Following these events, the Trudeau Government, who believed in multiculturalism, hired people to go across Canada and interview survivors in order to have historical records in Canada that would document the events that had taken place during the Holocaust. A man by the name of Josh Freed, a renowned broadcaster, came and interviewed me non-stop for about four and a half hours. He said that this story would be stored in archives both in Jerusalem and Ottawa. A few years later, I received a phone call from Allan Handle of the CBC, who told me they were making a documentary for the schools about the Holocaust and wanted to use my story, along with others. At his request, I loaned him some of my relevant pictures. The documentary that resulted was narrated by Stephen Lewis and was called *Voices of Survival*.

When I was living in Halifax and running my import business, one of my customers, Jim Goddard, who was also a friend, phoned me from St. Stephen, New Brunswick. I was expecting an order from him, but he had something else in mind. One of his friends, Larry Carter, a high school teacher in St. Stephen, had watched the CBC's *Voices of Survival* documentary and had discussed the events and people portrayed in the documentary with him. Jim told Larry Carter that he was a friend of one of the persons who was profiled in the documentary and that he would be willing to ask me if I would go to his school to speak to the students.

When Jim phoned me, I was surprised by his request. He presented it in the following manner: "Philip, I have known you for a long time, I buy from you, you shipped goods to me from Newfoundland, and now you have established yourself in Halifax. You never told me that you were a survivor of the concentration camps. It would be really helpful if you came to talk to students in the school here." My response to him was that I did not want to talk about it. However, he gently insisted and I thought about it for a while. A voice in my head told me that because I had survived I must go and speak out. Finally I decided to go, and that decision was to open up a whole new chapter of my life.

In 1989, I went to the St. Stephen High School to speak to three hundred students. It was the first time I was telling my story to an audience and I broke down in tears. However, I was not the only one. The students and teachers were touched by learning about the Holocaust and what it is like to be a survivor. Since then it has been like a snowball rolling in the snow. I speak wherever I am invited, in schools, universities, churches, in Canada as well as in the United States. Every time I tell something of my story, the emotions well up in me about the terrifying things I saw, and about the circumstances of my survival. I am reliving the horrors all over again because I cannot forget what no human being should ever experience and see. Sometimes I feel better after I have spoken, but I know that it is painful for others to hear. While they cannot fathom the depth of what it was like to be in these camps, they can empathize with me. It is one way to begin the journey of being informed, detect the falsehoods and heed the warnings of what could become another catastrophic conflict and attempt at genocide.

The reason I am speaking is because, when I look at these young people, I see myself when I was young like them. At that age I did not know what was going to happen to me. I survived, but millions and millions were killed by the evil deeds of Nazi-educated gangsters. There is no other nation on this planet that has been so brutal as to build gas chambers and crematoriums especially to murder families from town after town after town, until there was not even a name left—men, women and children, whole families, Jews, non-Jews, nobody. Wars are wars, but this kind of orgy of death is unthinkable. There are no words to describe fully these horrific deeds. Many times I feel like screaming, crying: *the world should know about it*. The Nazis combined efficiency with murderous intent to achieve their policies of a pure race and a Final Solution for exterminating Jews.

The younger generation should know what happened in that dark period of history. They have to make sure that their children and grandchildren know as well so that it can be prevented in the future. I want them to know how they can save themselves and their children. Because of our age, all survivors will soon be gone and someone else will have to pick up the challenge of talking about decency, love and hope that should exist between all human beings.

I keep being invited to speak again and again. Apart from the unrelenting nightmares, sometimes when I have to drive, all of a sudden sweat will come over me and I start to cry, often to the point of breaking down. Even when I am not out on a speaking engagement and I am sitting at home, the memories will overwhelm me and I cry for my family, my friends and all those who were victims of the Nazis' homicidal onslaught. It is beyond reason that people who did not fit the image of an acceptable race and had done nothing wrong should be brutality treated and murdered. Maybe I survived to speak out. I don't know. Something I know is that I have to spill it out and I make it my obligation to educate as many as I can so that they can make a difference in the world. Actually, a great number of students write to me and call me on the phone to tell me that I have changed their lives forever and want me to go and speak to other schools.

What I find very encouraging is that my presentation often spurs students and teachers to go further and do all kinds of projects, some very elaborate, about the Holocaust. They send me copies of what they have accomplished. An example of this work can be found in a young Cape Breton girl's decision to write a speech on the subject for a public speaking contest. Her name is Jennifer Morrison. She met with me and then with her speech went on to win first place in the contest, not only in her region, but at the

provincial level. And for this work she also was honoured with the Jerusalem Award. A little excerpt of the
speech reads as follows:

> *"As I sat there listening to Philip, I was eerily trans-
> ported through time until I felt I was right there during
> the time of the Nazi era."*

Another twelve-year-old student, Katie Poirier, voiced
her feelings in the following manner:

> *"Even though I can't even really understand or imagine
> what it was like, I could just almost feel that I was
> there."*

What is interesting is the fact that students who hear all
this realize that movies about the Holocaust represent
only the tip of the iceberg. Without the impact of a real
witness, students may not integrate their new knowledge in their world view or develop the necessary commitment to act against threats to the freedom of
humankind. One of the ways to get involved is to recognize that we owe our lives and our freedom to the Allies,
to those brave soldiers who fought Hitler's madness.
Soldiers need to be honoured with our presence at the
memorials on Remembrance Day. Too many brave men
gave their lives to fight the terrible war exacted by the
Nazi regime.

I have been doing these presentations for twenty years now. At the end of what I have to say, I always ask if there are any questions. It was in the early years at one of these presentations that an eleventh grade student asked me if Hitler had killed the Jews because they didn't believe in God. I was stunned. He thought that the majority of people on the earth were Christians. I felt obliged to tell him that there were many religions in our world and that these different spiritual beliefs do not give free rein for the killing of people. It was for me a troubling moment that convinced me of the importance of educating young people.

In appearance, one could say that I have a beautiful house, a lovely wife, children, and people that love me. But behind all this I am still a man walking a lonely valley with all these excruciating memories that will not go away. Even today, it is very hard to get dressed, go out to see people, and smile. In the back of my mind there is something else. I say to myself that these people I meet are very kind, but really they don't understand what I had to go through. They may feel my pain, but they can't understand the depth and scope of the tragedies I have experienced. I want to tell them that they are lucky that they were never occupied by people such as the Nazis.

When Memorial University of Newfoundland wrote me a letter and told me they wanted to give me an Honorary Doctoral Degree in Law, I was surprised and wondered why they would want to give me such a degree. A few people called me to ask me to accept this honour, and I did. I thanked them and appreciated it. Since then I have received a second Honorary Doctoral Degree from St. Thomas University in New Brunswick, the medal of the Order of Nova Scotia, and many other honours for the work I do. But I do not go on speaking to be honoured. When I look in the eyes of this younger generation I see that my testimony changes them in a most profound way. Perhaps it is because I put a face on this part of history and my presence as a real survivor telling my story, can help them better visualize what happened. Probably, this can make a stronger impression than books. I have received thousands of letters from students and teachers thanking me for opening their minds and letting them see how unbridled cruelty can lead to tragedies of apocalyptic proportions. In these letters there are recurrent themes as well: overwhelming emotions from hearing my life story, the importance of remembering the Holocaust, standing up for oneself, speaking out against racism and realizing that it is better to love than hate.

One thing I cannot explain to them is how persons who were living normal lives, having families, and even attending church, could suddenly turn into barbaric brutes and mass murderers. According to scholars, there are dangers that lurk in the dark side of human nature, especially in the context of strong authority. Evil deeds can be found in ordinary people. And we cannot forget two thousand years of anti-Semitism, conspiracy theories, racism, propaganda and, in the beginning of the twentieth century, the attribution of responsibility to the Jews for all of Germany's woes. However, I believe that this switch in human beings' behaviours has not yet been fully explored. Dr. Jekyll who becomes Mr. Hyde is still in our midst.

EPILOGUE

Message to the Younger Generation

I AM SPEAKING FOR MILLIONS and millions who cannot speak: Jews and non-Jews who died as a result of the Nazis' infamous, systematic and murderous practices during the Third Reich. I want the younger generation to know what happened. This part of history is important to remember because, if forgotten, there is a risk of it happening again and again.

When will we ever learn? This question reminds us all that, given particular conditions, human beings can commit acts of terrible evil against people and countries. I never thought it would happen to me. But it did, and it could happen again if we are not vigilant. When I go speaking in schools I feel like I am crying in the wilderness, I am crying to God, I am crying to young people so that they can be aware of the dangers of evil thinking and malicious intentions. I appeal to teachers to be open-minded and educate their students about the Holocaust. With this knowledge, the world may have a chance that it will not happen again. The hope for the world is in the young people who can acquire the skills to recognize brainwashing, demagoguery, propaganda and falsehoods through the development of critical thinking, the help of thoughtful teachers and serious reading. They can become shining lights in a dark world, standing up for what they believe, and fearing no one.

If the reason I survived was to tell the story in order to educate the younger generation, like other survivors have done, then the story needs to continue to be told after we have gone. Maybe millions and millions of souls are watching. The message I want to make known is one of Love rather than Hate. Hate destroys people, communities and countries. Love binds us all together and makes a better world.

Remember, it is better to Love than Hate.

Acknowledgements

I would like to express my gratitude to the American Army who liberated me in 1945 and brought me back to life.

To my three aunts, Celia Silver, Freida Wilansky, and Molly Block who joined forces so I might leave the displaced persons camp and join them in North America in 1946, I am most grateful.

To Judge William Joseph Browne, who facilitated bringing me to Newfoundland while Canada and the United States were slow to act, I owe a special thanks. To Jim Goddard who persisted in getting me to speak up. To the Atlantic Jewish Council, who aid, administer and support my educational efforts.

Finally, I owe a very special thank you to my wife, Dorothy, who has supported me tirelessly all these years.

The publisher wishes to thank Aurélien Bonin, Father William J. Browne, Adam Freake, Anne Hart, Edna LeVine, Helen Miller of the St. John's City Archives, and the United States Holocaust Memorial Museum.

Notes

1. Cyprys, Ruth Altbeker, *A Jump for Life: A Survivor's Journal from Nazi-Occupied Poland*. New York: Continuum 1997.

2. *Shershev*: the town of Shershev in the eastern part of Poland called Belarus was also known as Shereszów.

3. *Malch*: the town of Malch in the eastern part of Poland called Belarus was also known as Malecz.

4. *Pruzhany*: the town of Pruzhany in the eastern part of Poland called Belarus was also known as Pruzhana.

5. *Russians*: where Philip Riteman grew up in the town of Shershev, people of the Soviet Union were referred to as Russians.

6. Irving, Abella and Troper, Harold. *None Is Too Many: Canada and the Jews of Europe 1933-1948*. Toronto: Lester & Orpen Denys 1983.

PHILIP RITEMAN was born in Shershev in the Brest-Litvosk region of Poland. Forced from their town by the Germans in 1941, Philip and his family, along with thousands of other Jews, were deported into the Pruzhany ghetto. They were transported to Auschwitz in the winter of 1942. Philip's parents, brothers, and sisters were put to death in the gas chambers. Philip and two remaining brothers were selected for slave labour. From Auschwitz-Birkenau, Philip was sent to Sachsenhausen, Oranienburg, Dachau, and finally Landsberg. Liberated by the American Seventh Army in 1945, after crossing the Tyrolean Alps on a death march, Philip was the only member of his family to survive.

Philip sought to leave Europe and start a new life in North America. Only Newfoundland, an independent country at that time, was quick to respond in Philip's favour. In 1946 Philip began his new life as a door-to-door peddler in his new country. Visiting Montreal, Philip met and subsequently married Dorothy Smilestein, who joined him in St. John's. Their two sons are both graduates of Memorial University. In Newfoundland, Philip owned a wholesale dry goods business. By the time he left for Halifax in 1979, he had established a successful import trading company.

For many years, Philip did not speak about the Holocaust. In 1989, he gave testimony as a survivor for the first time at a school in St. Stephen, New Brunswick. He spoke to silence Holocaust deniers who claimed that the extermination of 6,000,000 Jews by the Germans had either never occurred or was greatly exaggerated. He spoke for those who could not speak.

For more than twenty years, Philip has continued to bear witness as a survivor. At schools, churches, universities, legion halls, and business enterprises throughout Canada and the United States, he has shared painful memories and a commitment to a more just society. For his contribution, Philip has been awarded honorary doctorates by Memorial and St. Thomas Universities as well as the Order of Nova Scotia.

MIREILLE BAULU-MACWILLIE obtained her Ph.D. from the Université de Montréal and dedicated her forty-five-year career to the field of education. In her first twenty-five years, she taught students at all academic levels: primary school, high school, and community college. She also held the administrative position of principal in a public school. She spent the last twenty years of her career at Université Sainte-Anne in Nova Scotia as a professor of education preparing students for the teaching profession. She has written many scholarly articles and two books, some of these in collaboration with colleagues.

She has had a lifelong interest in reading about Holocaust survivors and rescuers since the age of thirteen and tried to read every book or document she could find on the subject. She considers that the project of writing Philip Riteman's story has been a great responsibility, an extraordinary privilege, and a profoundly enriching experience. He was the first survivor she had ever met in person. She is grateful that he chose to let her write his story when he had been asked by others over the years to allow them this opportunity. She has developed an undying admiration and respect for Mr. Riteman's determination to survive and the courage to tell his story.

Appendix:
Photos

SURVIVOR - PHILIP RITEMAN

We cannot say,
We understand what he has gone through.

Every day he hears the screaming
Mercy cries of children.
Every day he sees the skeleton bodies,
Yearning for something to eat,
A glass of milk or piece of bread.
Every day he sees the brutal beatings
Of women and their babies.
Every day he remembers that his family
Is gone, torn away from him and murdered.
Every day he remembers the fear he felt
Not knowing if he would survive another day.
These are haunting memories of the Holocaust
That he shall not soon forget.

Brown hair or blond hair,
What difference does it make?
Freckles or no freckles,
What difference does it make?
Tall or short, thin or plump,
Black or white, young or old,
What difference does it make?
German or Jewish what difference . . .

To have been put through such hell,
Just because he is Jewish,
Is not fair or sane.

His life will be haunted forever.
Terrible memories, nauseating nightmares,
Cold sweats, and shaking.
No one can say,
"It's all right, you'll get over it.

MICHELLE NANTES

PHILIP RITEMAN'S FAMILY PRE—WORLD WAR II. Back row, standing (L-R): Philip's brother Aaron; his sister Liebe; and his brother Label. Centre row (L-R): Philip's mother, Rachel; his father, Lazer; and his little sister, Malka. Sitting on the floor (L-R): Philip Riteman; and his brother Shalom. Two other brothers do not appear in this photograph. Philip is the only survivor. All the other members of his family perished in Auschwitz. (Author photo)

Philip's grandparents Berger and a cousin who perished in Auschwitz. (Author photo)

Philip's father's brother, Fischel, and his wife, Basha, who perished in Auschwitz. (Author photo)

The children of one of Philip's father's sisters, who together with their parents perished in Auschwitz. (Author photo)

A first cousin of Philip's, on his mother's side,
who also perished in Auschwitz. (Author photo)

The children of another of Philip's father's sisters, who together with their
parents also perished in Auschwitz. (Author photo)

Philip's mother's brother Shalom Berger and his wife who perished in Auschwitz. (Author photo)

Philip's cousins, the children of his uncle Shalom, also perished in Auschwitz. (Author photo)

Unidentified members of Philip's extended family. This and other family photos were found in the houses of Philip's aunts in St. John's, Newfoundland, and Montreal, Quebec. His mother sent these family photos to her sisters before World War II. They are the only remaining evidence of Philip's family who died in the concentration camps. (Author photo)

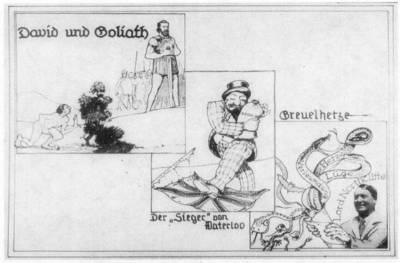

. . . propaganda against Jews extended to our area: "Hate the Jews! Hate the Jews!" Lamentably it caused people that had nothing against the Jews to start hating them. Germany, circa 1936. (United States Holocaust Memorial Museum, courtesy of Library of Congress)

A group of Jewish men are forced to stand with their arms raised in an unidentified Polish town. Poland, 1939–1940. (United States Holocaust Memorial Museum, courtesy of YIVO Institute for Jewish Research)

A German soldier laughs as three religious Jews are forced to remove their head coverings in public. Warsaw, Poland, 1939–1940. (United States Holocaust Memorial Museum, courtesy of Zydowski Instytut Historyczny imienia Emanuela Ringelbluma)

German police or soldiers check the identification papers of a Jew in the streets of Krakow. Krakow, Poland, 1940. (United States Holocaust Memorial Museum, courtesy of Archiwum Panstwowe w Krakowie)

A German policeman checks the identification papers of Jews in the Krakow ghetto. Krakow, Poland, circa 1941. (United States Holocaust Memorial Museum, courtesy of Archiwum Panstwowe w Krakowie)

Public hanging of Serbian civilians by German troops in the village of Uzicka Pozega, Serbia. Uzicka Pozega, Yugoslavia, 1941. (United States Holocaust Memorial Museum, courtesy of Muzej Revolucije Narodnosti Jugoslavije)

A German soldier points his rifle at a prisoner lying on the ground in the village Jajinci. The village of Jajinci near Belgrade served as an execution site for inmates from the Banjica concentration camp. Jajinci, Yugoslavia, 1941. (United States Holocaust Memorial Museum, courtesy of Muzej Revolucije Narodnosti Jugoslavije)

Dutch Jews wearing prison uniforms marked with a yellow star and the letter "N," for Netherlands, stand at attention during a roll call at the Buchenwald concentration camp. Buchenwald, Germany, February 28, 1941. (United States Holocaust Memorial Museum, courtesy of Gedenkstaette Buchenwald)

Men with an unidentified unit execute a group of Soviet civilians kneeling by the side of a mass grave. USSR, June 22–September 1941. (United States Holocaust Memorial Museum, courtesy of National Archives and Records Administration, College Park)

Sixteen blindfolded partisan youths await execution by German forces in Smederevska Palanka, Serbia. Executed with this group was a German soldier who refused to take part in the action. Smederevska Palanka, Yugoslavia, August 20, 1941. (United States Holocaust Memorial Museum, courtesy of Muzej Revolucije Narodnosti Jugoslavije)

Germans escort people from Kragujevac and its surrounding area to be executed. Kragujevac, Yugoslavia, October 1941. (United States Holocaust Memorial Museum, courtesy of Muzej Revolucije Narodnosti Jugoslavije)

German soldiers of the Waffen-SS and the Reich Labor Service look on as a member of an *Einsatzgruppen* prepares to shoot a Ukrainian Jew kneeling on the edge of a mass grave filled with corpses. Vinnitsa, Ukraine, 1941–1943. (United States Holocaust Memorial Museum, courtesy of Library of Congress)

A Serbian gendarme serving the Serbian puppet government led by Milan Nedic escorts a group of Gypsies to their execution. Yugoslavia, circa 1941–1943. (United States Holocaust Memorial Museum, courtesy of Muzej Revolucije Narodnosti Jugoslavije)

Captured Slovenian partisans are led by soldiers to their execution. Yugoslavia, 1941–1945. (United States Holocaust Memorial Museum, courtesy of Muzej Revolucije Narodnosti Jugoslavije)

Ustasa guards in the Jasenovac concentration camp strip newly arrived prisoners of their personal possessions. Jasenovac, Yugoslavia, August 1941–April 1945. (United States Holocaust Memorial Museum, courtesy of Jewish Historical Museum, Belgrade)

Ustasa guards move among a large group of Serbian villagers who are seated on the ground near the entrance to the Jasenovac concentration camp. Jasenovac, Yugoslavia, circa 1942. (United States Holocaust Memorial Museum, courtesy of Memorijalni muzej Jasenovac)

Executions of Kiev Jews by German army mobile killing units (*Einsatzgruppen*) near Ivangorod, Ukraine. The photo was mailed from the Eastern Front to Germany and intercepted at a Warsaw post office by a member of the Polish resistance collecting documentation on Nazi war crimes. The original German inscription on the back of the photograph reads, "Ukraine 1942, Jewish Action [operation], Ivangorod."

The body of a Soviet prisoner of war who committed suicide on an electrified barbed-wire fence in Mauthausen. Mauthausen, Austria, September 1942–October 1942. (United States Holocaust Memorial Museum, courtesy of National Archives and Records Administration, College Park)

Ustasa militia execute prisoners near the Jasenovac concentration camp. Jasenovac, Yugoslavia, 1942–1943. (United States Holocaust Memorial Museum, courtesy of Jewish Historical Museum, Belgrade)

SS guards walk along the arrival ramp at Auschwitz-Birkenau. Crematoria II and III can be seen in the far background. Auschwitz-Birkenau, Poland, May 1944. (United States Holocaust Memorial Museum, courtesy of Yad Vashem)

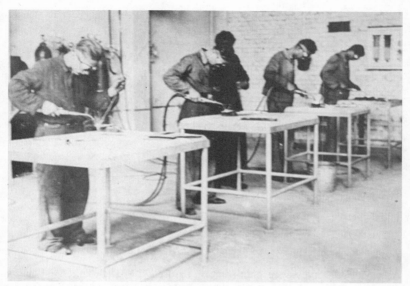

Forced labour in a workshop in Monowitz. Auschwitz, Poland. (United States Holocaust Memorial Museum, courtesy of National Archives and Records Administration, College Park)

Jewish women and children who have been selected for death walk in a line toward the gas chambers. Auschwitz, Poland, May 1944. (United States Holocaust Memorial Museum, courtesy of Yad Vashem)

An aerial reconnaissance photograph of Auschwitz II (Birkenau) showing crematoria IV and V, gas chambers and undressing rooms. Auschwitz, Poland, August 25, 1944. (United States Holocaust Memorial Museum, courtesy of National Archives and Records Administration, College Park)

Postwar view of the crematoria and gas chamber in Majdanek through the barbed-wire fence. Majdanek, Poland, after 1944. (United States Holocaust Memorial Museum, courtesy of Unknown Russian archive)

View of a row of barracks at the Kaufering IV concentration camp soon after the liberation. Hurlach, Germany, April 1945. (United States Holocaust Memorial Museum, courtesy of General Anthony McAullife, estate of)

An emaciated survivor drinking from a metal bowl in front of a barracks in Buchenwald. Buchenwald, Germany, April 11–June 1945. (United States Holocaust Memorial Museum, courtesy of National Archives and Records Administration, College Park)

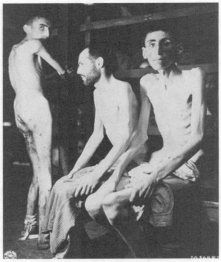

Three emaciated survivors in a barracks in the newly liberated Buchenwald concentration camp. Buchenwald, Germany, April 16, 1945. (United States Holocaust Memorial Museum, courtesy of National Archives and Records Administration, College Park)

The corpse of a prisoner lies on the barbed-wire fence in Leipzig-Thekla, a sub-camp of Buchenwald. Leipzig-Thekla, Germany, April 19, 1945–May 1945. (United States Holocaust Memorial Museum, courtesy of National Archives and Records Administration, College Park)

Railway cars loaded with the corpses of prisoners who died en route to Dachau from other concentration camps. The Dachau death train consisted of nearly forty railcars containing the bodies of between 2,000 and 3,000 prisoners who were evacuated from Buchenwald on April 7, 1945. The train arrived in Dachau on the afternoon of April 28. Dachau, Germany, April 30, 1945. (United States Holocaust Memorial Museum, courtesy of National Archives and Records Administration, College Park)

Prisoners' barracks in the Dachau concentration camp. Dachau, Germany, May 3, 1945. (United States Holocaust Memorial Museum, courtesy of National Archives and Records Administration, College Park)

Survivors of the Dachau concentration camp prepare to move a corpse during a demonstration of the cremation process at the camp. Dachau, Germany, May 4, 1945. (United States Holocaust Memorial Museum, courtesy of Muzeum Niepodleglosci)

A pile of corpses in the newly liberated Dachau concentration camp. Dachau, Germany, May 4, 1945. (United States Holocaust Memorial Museum, courtesy of Muzeum Niepodleglosci)

The door to the gas chamber in Dachau. It is marked "shower-bath." Dachau, Germany, July 1, 1945. (United States Holocaust Memorial Museum, courtesy of National Archives and Records Administration, College Park)

Two ovens inside the crematorium at the Dachau concentration camp. Dachau, Germany, July 1, 1945. (United States Holocaust Memorial Museum, courtesy of National Archives and Records Administration, College Park)

So this aunt from Newfoundland went to see William Joseph Browne the Judge in the Magistrate's Court and asked him about letting me come. His answer was, "By all means, right away." (Courtesy of Father William J. Browne)

After leaving me off in St. Pierre, I stayed in a hotel called Hôtel Robert for a week. They helped me recuperate, they fed me. Everybody used to come and see me there. (Courtesy of J.P. Andrieux)

CONVICTIONS

1.
Offence ....
Penalty imposed .... Sec. of Act violated ....
Signature of Magistrate ....
Date .... Address of Magistrate ....

2.
Offence ....
Penalty imposed .... Sec. of Act violated ....
Signature of Magistrate ....
Date .... Address of Magistrate ....

3.
Offence ....
Penalty imposed .... Sec. of Act violated ....
Signature of Magistrate ....
Date .... Address of Magistrate ....

4.
Offence ....
Penalty imposed .... Sec. of Act violated ....
Signature of Magistrate ....
Date .... Address of Magistrate ....

NEWFOUNDLAND 1947
DRIVER'S LICENCE 11885

Automobile.
Commercial Vehicle.
Public Service Vehicle.
Motor Cycle.
Traction Engine

Name *Philip Pittman*
Address *31 Topsail Rd.*
District

Whose ordinary signature is *Philip Pittman*

St. John's, *Aug 27* 1947.

J. S. NEILL,
Commissioner for Public Utilities

Form P.W. 53-14M-11-46 Dicks

Countersigned ....

Philip's first driver's licence, issued in Newfoundland in 1947. (Author photo)

156

Philip Riteman, when he was visiting family in Montreal, Quebec, in his late twenties. There he met his wife, Dorothy Smilestein. (Author photo)

The first weeks that I was in Newfoundland at my aunt and uncle's house, I used to help out in the store that they owned. This store was the largest jewellery store in St. John's. It was called Silver's Jewellery and it was comparable to the Birks jewellery store in Canada. (Courtesy of the City of St. John's Archives)

I was particularly close to one of their sons, Maurice Wilansky and his wife Sonya. They lived in St. John's. He and his wife had three children: Graham, Melvin, and Dorothy. My cousin realized that something was bothering me and he wanted to know how he could help me. I said to him: "All of you are so kind and good to me and want to help me, but I want to make it on my own." He was already established with a clothing store called Wilansky and Sons. (Courtesy of the City of St. John's Archives)

Philip Riteman. (Author photo)

Philip Riteman talking to students at Prince Andrew High School in Dartmouth, Nova Scotia.

Philip Riteman with the principal of a school at a presentation for students in Plymouth, New Hampshire.

STATE OF NEW HAMPSHIRE

HOUSE OF REPRESENTATIVES

A DECLARATION

Let it be known that
the New Hampshire House of Representatives,
on this occasion, publicly does recognize
and does grant its hearty and sincere congratulations to

Mr. Philip Riteman

In Recognition Of

*his exemplary and dedicated service in
educating the public about the Holocaust*

And be it further known that
the New Hampshire House of Representatives,
by virtue of the Speaker's signature inscribed below,
also does duly extend its highest accolades and plaudits.

Gene G. Chandler
Speaker of the House

Offered by Representatives Mary Cooney and Deb Nato this 21st day of May 2002

In 2002, the State of New Hampshire presented a certificate of recognition and thanks to Philip Riteman for his ongoing role in educating younger generations on the Holocaust. (Author photo)

Top Left: Philip Riteman receiving an honorary doctorate of laws at Memorial University in St. John's, Newfoundland, in 2006. Top Right and Bottom: Philip Riteman receiving an honorary doctorate of letters at St. Thomas University in Fredericton, New Brunswick, in 2008.

Philip Riteman receiving the 2009 Order of Nova Scotia.

SURVIVORS OF THE
SⁿHĸOₗAῳH
VISUAL HISTORY FOUNDATION.

3 December 1996

Philip Riteman
6 Eagle Place
Bedford, NS B4A 2J4
Canada

Dear Mr. Riteman,

In sharing your personal testimony as a survivor of the Holocaust, you have granted future generations the opportunity to experience a personal connection with history.

Your interview will be carefully preserved as an important part of the most comprehensive library of testimonies ever collected. Far into the future, people will be able to see a face, hear a voice, and observe a life, so that they may listen and learn, and always remember.

Thank you for your invaluable contribution, your strength, and your generosity of spirit.

All my best,

Steven Spielberg
Chairman

MAIN OFFICE · POST OFFICE BOX 3168 · LOS ANGELES, CALIFORNIA 90078-3168 PHONE 818.777-7802 FAX 818.733-0312

In 1996, filmmaker Steven Spielberg (*Schindler's List*) sent Philip Riteman a letter of thanks and congratulations on his continuing efforts to preserve the memory of the Holocaust. (Author photo)

Philip and Dorothy Riteman on stage speaking to Canadian troops.

PHILIP RITEMAN'S FAMILY TODAY. (L-R): Philip; his wife, Dorothy; their son Robert; and their son Larry. (Author photo)

Index